For Mark,

Enjoy the

No Ordinary Dad

By Fiona Barrett

Best wishes

Fiona

First Published in 2024

Printed in Great Britain

About the Author

Fiona works part-time as a nurse and lives in Berkshire with her husband, Nigel, and their beloved working cocker, Lulu. She has four children, the youngest of whom has recently flown the nest for university, leaving Fiona time to pursue her dream of writing *'No Ordinary Dad.'*

Dedication

Heartfelt thanks to our wonderful Scottish clan for welcoming us into your lives with open arms, with neither prejudice nor judgement. Also, in memory of Ellen and Sam, we were so glad we got to meet you, and to David; we wish we'd found you all sooner.

Acknowledgment

I'd like to say a special thanks to Stuart Ogilvie for sharing his story and photograph of his beloved Aunt Agnes. A huge thank you to Darren Treadwell, an archivist at the People Museum in Manchester, for patiently finding the answers to my endless requests for information, and to Melissa Edwards, the wonderful genealogist who compiled an ancestry report for us on our grandfather's family after we had come to a dead end. We were to discover from her report that, for some reason, our great-grandfather had changed our surname from Branigan to Brunton! Quite why he did that we shall never know. To my wonderful husband, Nigel, who gave up his weekends and even his birthday to sit looking through dusty old records with me and who has supported me for the three months I took off work to finally get this all down on paper. A huge thanks to my boss, Lucy Sullivan, for giving me my three-month sabbatical. To my dear friend Jo Rickard for proofreading and editing all of my errors. Also, a big thank you to Julietta Wilson-Tromp for her honest review and for recommending the epilogue to tie up loose ends. Finally, the biggest thank you of all goes to Bev for all the years of painstaking research she put into finally finding our Scottish clan family!

"Lying by omission is when a person leaves out important information or fails to correct a pre-existing misconception in order to hide the truth from others."

—The Urban Dictionary

Blank page left intentionally

Table of Contents

CHAPTER 1: 2.4 KIDS

Like most kids, I had never given a thought about my parents having a life before I was born; they were just Mum and Dad. I'd never considered that they might have actually led quite interesting lives before having us children. Growing up, there was me, my sister Bev, who is almost seven years older than me, plus Mum and Dad. We'd grown up in the Ellesmere Port and Chester area, with Mum working locally as a part-time practice nurse and Dad working for British Engineer Insurance as a safety metal inspector. We lived in Dawn Gardens in Ellesmere Port for the first four years of my existence, a small cul-de-sac on the outskirts of the town. The house was a modern terrace with a garden that backed onto a huge park. I can just about remember standing in the garden watching a May Day celebration fete and donkeys being led around the perimeter of the park, carrying young children, and me squeezing my little hands through the fence trying to touch the donkeys. It was a friendly cul-de-sac with several young families, and at the bottom was a newsagent where Dad would buy his paper and Virginia tobacco for his pipe. He bought me my very own green pipe when I was about ten, though it never had any tobacco in it obviously. I remember the shop owner used to call me 'half pint' because I was so short for my age – I still am! To be fair, I didn't stand a chance, as both Mum and Dad were about five feet, eight inches tall, Dad being on the short side for a man and Mum being considered quite tall for a woman.

Opposite the shop was the Salvation Army Citadel, which was a big part of our early lives. Whilst my Mum was not a member, her sister, Aunty Ethel, and her own mother were. Some weekday afternoons were spent there at the over-sixties club attended by our maternal grandma and her two best friends and partners in crime, Nell and Flo. Mum and Aunty Ethel would be handing out tea and biscuits, and I would be running round having my cheeks pinched and playing with the children of other 'army' members.

Mum had been raised as part of the 'army' family, along with her parents and siblings, until she started nursing terminally ill children at Leasowe Children's Hospital. After working there and witnessing the suffering the children endured, she lost her faith and left the army as a member but continued to help out on occasion whilst her own mother was still alive. When Grandma died in 1976, she never attended the citadel again other than for family weddings.

The best years of my childhood were spent living in Saughall, where we moved to when I was four years old, a village four miles or so from Chester and very close to the Welsh border. In fact, the village football pitch had one goal in England and the other in Wales, and it could rain just at one end. I can remember the day we moved into our newly built home. On the floor were lots of round metal discs, some sort of leftover bits of building material, left by the builders, and I went round picking them all up, thinking it was money.

Saughall is a very old village, mentioned in the Domesday Book of 1086 when it was known as Salhale. When we moved there in 1971, it had a population of just under two and a half thousand but was rapidly expanding as new housing estates were being quickly built to meet rising demand. Throughout the new estates, the street lights were run on gas, so a man used to come every evening to light them individually. I would kneel on my bed, watching out of the window as he progressed along the road, patiently lighting each one.

There were several shops, my favourite being Whaley's sweet shop run by old Mrs Whaley and her daughter-in-law. It had an old wooden counter and there were huge jars of sweets that lined the shelves right up to the ceiling. Young Mrs Whaley had a sliding ladder to reach those jars at the top, whilst old Mrs Whaley was always behind the counter and sat in her rocking chair. Tuesdays were my treat days, and my grandma would give me sixpence to buy my favourites, the lemon bon bons, small and round, dusted with sweet icing sugar and then the sharp taste of lemon in the middle.

The village was surrounded by farms where our parents would buy their eggs and potatoes, and where I would play in the fields, climb trees, and build dens. I attended the local school, Thomas Wedge, where the toilets were outside and accessed via a cobbled alley, a throwback to its Victorian days. Going to the toilet in the winter was freezing, and you risked the locks on the doors being frozen, so you'd be locked in the cubicle and banging and shouting for help for ages until someone realised you were missing from class and came to find you.

In the summer holidays, the school ran a summer playscheme, similar to today's holiday camps, and we would go with the teachers to explore the nearby Bluebell woods to look at the wildlife. I remember going on a twilight badger and bat trail one summer's evening, keeping very quiet, as instructed, with just the moonlight to guide us. That was the only time I have ever seen live badgers. The woods were opposite Shotwick Park, a stunning red brick Victorian building set within seven acres of beautiful woodland with its own tennis courts. There was a fearsome gamekeeper who patrolled the area, with a shotgun under his arm, and he would chase us if he ever caught us sneaking into the woods. The house itself was once a private home designed by architect John Douglas for Horace Dormer Trelawney, an army captain in the Royal Horse Guards. These days, it has been converted into houses. Footballer John Barnes had a house here; buying one now would cost you over £600,000. Back in the 1970s when we were kids, it was a nursing home. I can remember watching Eric, one of the residents, sitting ever so still on one of the many wooden benches, whilst balancing nuts on his shoe, and the red squirrels would come and take the food from his foot.

It was a very happy childhood, attending the village school, swimming lessons on a Saturday morning at the local pool, ballroom dancing lessons in the village hall, and playing outside until it was time to come home for tea. Whilst it was ideal for me, it was maybe not so great for Bev; being that much older meant that her social credibility was sometimes challenged as she was often told she had to babysit the annoying little sister.

My bedroom was downstairs and at the front of the house, and on many a Saturday night, I could be seen peeking out of the window, earwigging on Bev and her friends who would hang out on the front garden wall. In a bid to stop me from getting out of bed, she would tell me the Bogeyman would come and get me. This threat massively backfired one evening when she missed the last bus home and I awoke to the sound of gentle tapping on my bedroom window. I was out of bed and up the stairs to Mum and Dad's room, screaming like a banshee, believing the Bogeyman had actually come for me.

That house in The Ridings in Saughall was a kaleidoscope of colours. After staying in a hotel and admiring their carpets, Dad decided we too were in need of a tartan carpet. He had a truly hideous, but apparently very expensive, red and yellow tartan carpet put in the hallway

4

right up the stairs and across the landing. Bev's bedroom was several shades of brown, Mum and Dad's was green, and we had the classic aqua-marine blue bathroom suite. Not long afterwards, Mum went into hospital to have her gallbladder removed and, as a surprise for her, Dad painted the entire house her favourite colour, lilac.

In July 1976, when I was nine years old, Dad went out to work for several months in Pyongyang, North Korea, as an inspector at a chemical plant for non-destructive metal testing. It was not a smooth journey by all accounts; for the first leg of it, he had to fly out from London to Moscow. Shortly after landing, Mum received a phone call from the British Embassy telling her not to worry, but Dad had been arrested for not having the right paperwork. After a night spent in a police cell, the correct paperwork was finally produced from British Engineer Insurance. The drama did not end there; the second leg of the journey was from Moscow to Peking flying Russian Aeroflot, where the plane landed in the middle of an earthquake! Never being one to follow the rules, rather than presenting himself to the British Embassy as advised, Dad was actually classed as missing, only to be found in a hotel bar sipping a whisky with a fellow Scot! Well, it must've been pretty scary to experience! Whilst out there, Dad wrote back home regularly from his segregated accommodation in the 'Foreigners Building' called 'Stalag 2'. Mum still has many of these letters. In one, he recalls being hailed a celebrity for having the honour of meeting and having his photo taken with Kim Il-sung, founder of North Korea, who ruled from 1948 until his death in 1994, and who happened to be introduced to Dad when he visited the chemical plant Dad was working at.

In another of these letters, he recalls trying to teach the local chef at the staff accommodation how to make bacon and eggs for his breakfast. The Koreans didn't generally eat hot food, so the chef would kindly make Dad's breakfast and then put the plate outside to go nice and cold for him.

Dad was a very eloquent letter writer, and despite his humble background, he could recite Shakespeare and Rabbie Burns with ease and knew many poems by heart, including rude ones! One of my favourites being:

Anklers sausages are the best

In your tummy they do rest

Down the toilet they do lie

Pull the chain and watch them fly.

Another of his repertoire was a children's Scottish tenement song called 'Aunty Mary Had a Canary!'

Aunty Mary had a canary up the leg of her drawers,

When she farted out it darted to a round of applause

She pulled a string to make it sing

And down came Santa Claus

When she was sleeping, it was creeping

Up the leg of her drawers

I remember the excitement of going to pick him up from Manchester airport and seeing him come down the escalators after being away for so many months. He was laden with gifts of Russian dolls and two beautiful traditional Korean silk outfits for Bev and me; a gold one for me, a silver one for Bev. He was only home for three months before heading back out there for another long stint. I remember feeling very important at school as the headmaster, Mr Clark, a fellow Scot, would sometimes invite me into his office and give me milk and biscuits and ask me all about Dad and what he was doing in Korea. I now suspect the reason for those nice chats was to find out what Dad was up to and because Mr Clark's own political leanings were similar to Dad's. When Dad returned that second time he brought back Cholera and we were all quarantined by Public Health England.

The next job Dad had after this was in Peterborough, working for SodaStream Ltd. I gained great kudos amongst my friends as we had one of these amazing machines that produced fizzy drinks like Cola and Irn-Bru. Whilst living up there in Peterborough Monday to Friday, he lodged with Mary and Sandy who were to become lifelong friends. So much so that we even went to stay with them whilst they were on holiday up in Glen Lyon in Scotland. I remember the rented house being very isolated and sat on the banks of the River Lyon where Sandy spent many hours teaching me how to tickle the belly of the salmon as they basked in the shallow waters and how to then flip them out onto the river bank. Next to the house was a fence with a stile in it for crossing into the surrounding countryside. At the base of the stile was a huge rock with a footprint in it. I remember Sandy telling me it must be Jesus's footprint as only God could have created something as beautiful as the Scottish Glens. I can still picture the forty shades of gold, as Dad called them, as the sun set over the mountains in the summer evenings.

Dad's role at SodaStream was to check the safety of the gas canisters used in the machines. It was whilst working there in 1979 that Dad had a car accident, hitting a young man on his bicycle, causing him to have a punctured lung.

Dad was absolutely devastated, calling the hospital daily to check on the chap's condition. Thankfully, he went on to make a full recovery. The police were involved, and it was realised that Dad did not actually have a driver's licence and had been driving illegally for years, and so that was the end of him driving. Passing a driving test for those that began driving after the 1st of April 1934 only became law in the UK in 1935, by which time Dad had already been driving for a few years. Over the years, he had many different cars; we often had no idea where they came from. My favourite was the Maxi Princess that had tables that pulled down from the back of the front seats, considered to be very sophisticated back in the 1970s. It was when he was driving one of these cars that Dad hit a pheasant; not being the type to waste anything, he brought it home for Mum to pluck and cook. Being the daughter of a game shop owner, Mum was proficient at skinning and prepping anything from a rabbit to, well, a pheasant. The feathers of that thing were stuck in the radiator grill of the car for weeks afterwards.

At one point, we had a VW caravanette that we had many family holidays in, travelling up to Rhosneigr in Anglesey to camp in a field near our Aunty Eileen's house. It had a roof space that popped up, and there were two bunks up there where Bev and I slept. I remember falling out and landing on Mum and Dad who were asleep underneath, scaring the living daylights out of them both. It was during one holiday up there that I fell, whilst being the ball boy during a game of tennis, running for the ball and falling over the wire holding the net up, knocking myself out in the process. Bleeding quite badly from a head injury, Bev carried me to Aunty Eileen's house where she handed me over to Mum before promptly fainting to the floor. She's never been good at the sight of blood, then or now.

After the car accident, Dad took to travelling by train up to Peterborough every Sunday evening, returning home on a Friday night. He often fell asleep on the train back to Peterborough and would miss his stop, waking up in London where the train terminated, and then would have to get another train back up to Peterborough.

I still feel guilty about having once forgotten my packed lunch for school and being told by friends that my Dad was at the school gates with it. He had taken two buses from Saughall to Chester and then out to Upton to get it to me, and I recall all he got was a grunt of thanks from twelve-year-old me before I dashed off to rejoin my friends.

He would arrive home on Friday evenings with a plastic bag bulging with Fry's chocolate and walnut whips. I loved them but always had to take the walnuts off the top; I still can't bear the taste of those nuts. If I had friends over, he would have us all hold our hands out and he would literally empty his pockets of coins and tip some into everybody's cupped hands. He was a gregarious and fun Dad whereas Mum was quite shy and would be in the background at the frequent parties held at our house. There's an infamous family tale about how, at a New Year's Eve party, the hinges on the pull-down drinks unit gave way, causing all the bottles to fall off and smash but Dad managed to lunge forwards, catching the only bottle of whisky which he alone drank. During these parties, I was made to sleep upstairs in Bev's room but would sneak out and spy on the partygoers through the bannisters until Dad caught me and kindly brought me a cup of drinking chocolate to 'help me sleep.' I suspect some of that whisky made it into that cup as I did indeed feel sleepy soon afterwards.

A year or so later, when I was twelve years old and Bev was at Bristol Poly, Mum and Dad announced that we were leaving Saughall and moving into Chester. I was gutted and really did not want to move. I had just started senior school and was unhappy about leaving my village school friends. It seemed an abrupt decision. In hindsight, I now know that Dad's bosses at Whessoe, where he went to work after leaving SodaStream, and for whom he had worked for many years before, had finally realised that Dad had been lying about his age and was, in fact, beyond the age of retirement. He was always a bit cagey about his age, so much so that even on his headstone, Mum chose not to put his date of birth on it, only the date he died, as he would have requested had he been of sound mind. Not only that, but because of Dad's communist beliefs, he had never paid into a pension, so money became a big issue for them. Apparently, Dad had never been 'good' with money, so it was Mum who took care of all the family finances. I recall there being a large metal tin with a key to lock it, that was divided into sections labelled 'gas,' 'telephone,' 'electricity,' etc., that she kept in the wardrobe in their bedroom. Mum made sure there was always enough for them to have a decent social life. As I recall, they were often out at a 'dance' or some other social event with friends most weekends. It had never occurred to me that Dad was almost twenty years older than Mum. In fact, he had been fifty-two when I was born.

BEV

I found it really weird that they were going to move, although Mum and Dad were great. They were stuck choosing between two houses, the one in Lorne Street and one in Hoole, and they wanted to see which I preferred, so they asked me to come up and see both houses with them. I said that I didn't really mind, it was completely up to them. However, it was really strange.

I returned from Bristol, and in the meantime, they had packed up everything and moved. I never got the chance to take a last look at my bedroom or house. Shortly after they had all moved, I remember getting off the train from Bristol on a surprise visit to their new home. I jumped into a taxi and excitedly told the driver that I was back from college for the weekend to surprise my family. He asked me for the address and then gave me the weirdest look as I suddenly realised that I didn't actually know their new address or their new number! I had to get back out and use a phone box to ring our aunty and ask her for the address!

We moved into a large, five-bedroomed Victorian terrace house in Lorne Street, walking distance from Chester city centre, in what was known as 'bedsit land' owing to the many multi-occupancy houses in the area. Mum and Dad used a bridging loan to buy it, keeping the Saughall house for several years afterwards as a rental property to provide another source of income. I hated going back there with Mum on rent day and seeing strangers in my childhood home. Lorne Street had a large garden, and Bev and I had a huge bedroom each in the cellar with an archway dividing the two rooms. My room had the only tiny window and also the central heating boiler, so it was toasty in winter and cool in the summer. The plan was for Dad to run the house as a B&B whilst Mum continued to work part-time as a nurse in Ellesmere Port.

The plus side to the move was that we were finally allowed to get a dog. Ailsa Craig, the West Highland Terrier, came into our lives and became Dad's constant companion. My life became a routine of school during the week and helping with bed changes and food shopping for guests at weekends. All to be done before I was allowed to hang out with friends. They were fun years, the house always full of different people from all over the world. Most summers we had foreign exchange students that would stay for weeks at a time attending an English language school in the city. I made good friends with many of them and fell in love with French boys regularly. There were moments of hilarity like the time we had three Libyan guests staying and they were sharing a meal with us. We were all sitting at the dining table when Ailsa appeared at the door and had clearly been digging in the wet earth outside. Without engaging my brain, I blurted out, 'Ailsa, you dirty little Arab, get out now!' I can't recall if it was Mum or Bev that legged it out to the kitchen first. They then spent the next ten minutes taking it in turns to stick their heads in the kitchen cupboard in an attempt to muffle their somewhat hysterical laughter. Meanwhile, I'm in the dining room saying, 'What? What is it? What are you doing?'

When Ailsa was four months old, she became very poorly with canine parvovirus, which is often fatal. She was being kept at the vet's practice whilst they did all they could to keep her alive. Dad was very upset, understandably. One evening, about midnight, I popped my head into my parents' bedroom to say goodnight and tried to reassure Dad that she was a little fighter and would pull through. He smiled at me and said, 'I know, she's okay and she'll be back home soon.' I asked if he had heard from the vet; he replied that he hadn't, he just had a 'feeling' that all was well. Dad believed that everyone had a sixth sense but that some people learned how to use it more than others. He had a few books on the subject that sat alongside his copies of books about Chairman Mao, the Chinese communist revolutionary, head of The Communist Party in China from 1949 until his death in 1976. Dad had an eclectic taste in books. The following morning, the vet rang to say Ailsa had 'turned the corner' and was likely to make a full recovery. I heard my Dad ask the vet roughly what time it was that she seemed to improve. 'Just before midnight' came the reply.

It was around this time that Dad started having strange episodes where he appeared to just 'blank out' for a few seconds at a time. There were other little changes happening too. If he and Mum went shopping, he would ask her to write the cheques, claiming to have misplaced his glasses. Looking back, there were times when he was working in Peterborough and he would wear his kilt for the journey. This was unusual as he only ever wore it for formal occasions such as weddings, but at the time he must have given what seemed a plausible explanation for wearing it on a train to work. He started to lose the ability to find the right words and was becoming increasingly frustrated. After much prompting and nagging from Mum, he allegedly went to see the general practitioner and came back saying there was nothing wrong, he was obviously just a bit stressed. There was clearly much more to it than just stress. On several occasions, Dad had taken Ailsa out for a walk only for the dog to return home alone. Bless that little dog, she would then lead you to where she had left him. Twice I found him on the Roodee racecourse looking lost and bewildered with no idea where he was or how long he'd been there.

Eventually, it became apparent that something was clearly very wrong, and he was admitted to Walton Hospital in Liverpool for investigations. The results of a brain scan were devastating. Dad had Alzheimer's disease. He was sixty-eight years old.

BEV

At this time, Alzheimer's disease did not have the public awareness that it does now. In fact, the Alzheimer's Disease Society, then headed by Sir Jonathan Miller, was only founded three or four years earlier. Respite care and support barely existed, but the society increased that dramatically during the period that Dad suffered. I remember the consultant at the hospital showing us the brain scan of a patient with age-related dementia and the one of Dad's brain with Alzheimer's. It was dramatically different, dementia being a general shrinkage of the brain around the edges, whereas Alzheimer's brains have random black patches throughout the brain where the cells have died. We learnt that this is why it affects people differently during the relentless progression of this cruel disease. Dad lost his ability to speak coherently relatively early on, but was able to read for comparatively much longer.

Top – Family holiday in Cornwall

Middle – Dad with his beloved Alisa on a caravan holiday in Tenby

Bottom – Our Mum and Dad

CHAPTER 2: THE IMPACT OF DEMENTIA

Life changed for us all after the diagnosis. We had never heard of this disease, and what we were learning was terrifying. Dad's deterioration was slow and steady. He would get angry and frustrated and shout at the TV. Poor Trevor McDonald got yelled at most nights as Dad believed he was talking directly to him. The loss of speech was getting worse, and he took to whistling to get our attention. Slowly, the ability to dress himself also went. Imagine the brain is like a pizza divided up into slices. Each slice represents a bodily function or ability, and then each slice becomes mouldy until the slice that controls breathing rots away, and all you're left with is the empty box. I remember one evening seeing him sitting on the edge of the bed in front of the mirror trying to put his tie on. He looked at my reflection, weeping and said, 'Please just let me die.' I was fifteen years old, and that memory is forever imprinted on my eyelids. He took to following Mum around the house everywhere, terrified of losing sight of her. Family and friends began to fade away; we were no longer invited to the Christmas dinners, and people we thought were friends would cross the street rather than talk to us.

On more than one occasion, I was walking with him and almost didn't pull him back when he would forget to check the road was clear before crossing. We were all struggling in our own way. I was embarrassed and ashamed to bring friends back to the house for fear of what he might do. He had started to urinate in kitchen cupboards, unable to remember where the bathroom was. There were many times I would be locked in my bedroom, literally all day. The cellar door had a snib lock on it, and you had to close the cellar door in order to open the door to the back garden. Nine times out of ten, Dad would subconsciously slide the snib across when opening the back door to let Ailsa out to the garden. Eventually, I had to put a bucket in the cellar to pee in on trapped days. By now, I was at Crewe College studying social care and would often get home to find a friend asleep on my bed. Having rung the front doorbell, they would be shown downstairs to the cellar by Dad, believing that's where I was, only to find themselves forgotten about and locked in.

At this time, I had a boyfriend, Jonny, whom Dad was very fond of. For years afterwards, any boyfriend I was brave enough to bring home got called Jon by Dad. It caused me many awkward moments over the years.

One day, I came down the road to see a fire engine parked outside our house and firemen going in through the front door. Fearing the worst, I ran in to find several of them drilling the bottom step off the flight of stairs leading down to my bedroom. Poor Ailsa had managed to get herself stuck under the house via a missing air brick and somehow Dad had managed to call for the fire service. For many nights afterwards, I would forget about that missing step and fall into my bedroom.

One day when I was seventeen, I had decided not to go into college; I can't remember why not. I was downstairs in my bedroom when I heard a thud above. I ran upstairs and found Dad unconscious on the lounge floor. Mum and Bev had gone out for the day. I rang for an ambulance, which arrived in minutes, by which time Dad had started to come round. I remember the paramedics loading him onto the ambulance and them asking him lots of questions, and me having to explain to them that he couldn't understand their questions because he had Alzheimer's disease. They had never heard of it, and I had to explain to them what it was.

Sadly, although awareness of this cruel disease is widespread, there is still no cure.

So, there were times when we did laugh when there was just nothing else you could do. I came home one day, and Dad started gesturing to me to go outside in an excited way. Upon opening one of the outhouse doors, I was confronted by a tiny kitten. Apparently, a policeman had found it and after knocking on several neighbours' doors got to our house where my Dad proclaimed it was ours. Mum hates cats with a passion, so I had to keep the poor thing hidden for two days whilst I found it a permanent home.

Another time, I came home to find a nice lady wheeling my bike away and thanking Dad profusely. He had just given it to her! That was my mode of transport for my Saturday job; by the time I then had to pay for a bus ride, it hardly made the job worthwhile.

Before long, it became evident that Dad was no longer safe to be left home alone, and so Ann came into our lives. Lovely, kind, calm Ann was a godsend and relieved the pressure off Mum hugely. She came in to sit with Dad whilst Mum was at work and made sure he ate and used the bathroom. She was incredibly patient and seemed genuinely fond of Dad, and more importantly, he seemed to like her too. She was with us for several years, and I still see her on the odd occasion when I visit Chester. Mum was still working part-time as well as running the B&B and caring for Dad. It was all getting too much. He started to attend a day centre in Hoole a couple of times a week to give Mum a break. There was one chap there who also had Alzheimer's; he was only thirty-two years of age.

At nineteen years old, I moved to Liverpool to start my nurse training, returning home on my days off to help

Mum. How she was still coping with everything, I do not know. Reluctant to give up her job, as this was her only means of an escape to 'normality', she soldiered on. She never told anyone in her workplace what was happening at home. It was only when Dad was eventually admitted to hospital for the last time that any of her work colleagues knew he had Alzheimer's.

In the early summer of 1990, Bev convinced Mum that she was in desperate need of a holiday, and so Dad went into the Countess of Chester Hospital for two weeks' respite care. He had previously been to the Cottage Hospital in Ellesmere Port, where Mum had worked as a newly qualified nurse, but they were no longer able to provide the care he needed. Ruth and Sandra were the two nursing sisters, and Steve was Dad's personal nurse on Selby ward. Steve remains a friend to this day. He told us later that the experience he had with us, as a family, during this time led him to pursue another vocation, as a vicar. I think Dad would have found that highly amusing. The care and compassion they showed, not just to Dad but to the three of us, was immeasurable. They even used to let us take Ailsa onto the ward so Dad could see her. Both nursing sisters and Steve would sometimes call at our home address to see how we were all coping. They were astonished that Mum had been caring for Dad for so long with so little support. The main personal support we got was from the local Alzheimer's Disease Society group and Mum's two great friends, Micky and Marg, who would sit with Dad whilst Mum and I attended support meetings or if Mum wanted to do something 'normal' like get a haircut. They were simply fabulous, and she misses them both dearly. It was through the local support group that Mum was approached by the Panorama programme, who were looking to film with a young family who had a family member with Alzheimer's, for which we fitted the criteria. Mum eventually decided not to go ahead with the filming, feeling it was going to be too intrusive for her.

At the end of May 1990, Dad seemed to have some sort of seizure. Mum took him back to the hospital as Bev and I were at work. He was re-admitted back onto Selby ward. To the hospital, it was probably very obvious that he could no longer be cared for at home; in fact, they were surprised that he had been admitted directly from the family home. Mum rang Bev in tears. She was just not ready to accept that and was distraught, saying, 'They won't let me have him back home and he won't cope without me.' It was one of the saddest moments since the nightmare had begun. A few days later, we arrived on the ward to visit Dad. Previously, he had been in bed when we arrived. This time, a member of staff had taken him to the loo and we were asked to take a seat whilst they got him back into bed. Seconds later, he came out of the bathroom with the nurse and glanced across at us... and there was no recognition whatsoever. This was the defining moment when Mum finally realised that he had no idea who she was.

He ended up staying on Selby ward for six weeks before passing away, with the three of us by his side, on Thursday, 5 July 1990, at five p.m. He was seventy-four years old.

The way in which Bev and I were treated by our respective bosses at this time could not have been more different. Bev's bosses at the brokerage firm insisted she took a minimum of three weeks off work and sent her a beautiful bouquet of flowers. My bosses, those in the 'caring' profession, bombarded me with daily phone calls demanding that I return to work immediately.

Like in life, his death was hardly conventional. I can still remember the baffled look on Mr Parry, the funeral director's face, as Mum explained that what she would really like to do with Dad's body was to drive it up to the Scottish Glens he loved so much and leave it there. When poor Mr Parry asked what religious denomination Dad was, he looked even more uncomfortable when Mum told him that we wouldn't require any religious figures at all; we merely wanted to hire the crematorium for an hour and do everything ourselves. She got her way, and I admire her for sticking to her guns and giving Dad the funeral he would've wanted. No mention of any God or a heaven and no stranger spouting that Dad had been 'a pillar of his community' whilst having never even met him. The funeral itself was both funny and sad, with friends getting up to tell funny stories they remembered about Dad. The story of Dad catching the whisky bottle was retold to much laughter. The commonality of all the stories was that of a generous and kind man with a great sense of humour.

A poignant moment was a lone bagpiper playing 'Amazing Grace' as the curtains slipped around his coffin. A fitting farewell to a proud Scotsman.

His ashes are buried in our maternal grandparents' burial plot in Overpool Road cemetery in Ellesmere Port. A very generous patient of mine donated the stone plaque on which we had inscribed a line from a song by Andy Stewart, one of Dad's favourite singers. It says, simply, 'Sleep in peace our Scottish laddie, now the battle's o'er.'

I felt great angst at the thought of Dad being cremated. I didn't see how you could be sure the ashes you got back were those of your loved one. I shared my concerns at work one day with Sam Pratt, the hospital chaplain. He and I would have great debates on the meaning of life and whether God exists or not. Two days after our talk I came into work and he told me he had arranged for me to spend the day behind the scenes at Liverpool Crematorium so I could see for myself the process of cremation. Whilst it sounds rather macabre it was a fascinating place and I was totally reassured that the ashes we buried in Overpool Road cemetery are indeed entirely our Dad's.

Such was my respect for Sam Pratt that when Nigel and I got married in 1993 I asked him to conduct part of our wedding ceremony. He kindly obliged despite knowing that I was only getting married in a church because it was important to Nigel and that I had no religious beliefs at all.

As Dad had died three years prior to me getting married, I asked Mum if she would do the honour of walking me down the aisle, all a bit controversial at the time but it was what I wanted and she agreed to it. As I've mentioned before, she was much quieter than Dad and she did baulk at the thought of making a wedding speech to a crowded room, but she did it and was fabulous. I was very proud of her and love to look at the photographs of the two of us on that special day.

CHAPTER 3: THE FIRST CLUE

It was whilst Dad was still in hospital having tests in Liverpool that I overheard Mum on the phone to Aunty Lena, our Dad's sister, who lived in Scotland.

'If the kids want to see him, they best come now before he gets worse,' I heard her say. Kids? What kids? I crept downstairs to Bev's room and whispered what I had just heard. We were completely nonplussed but were unwilling to actually confront Mum with what I'd heard.

Instead, we decided to write a letter to Aunty Lena, asking her to explain. A couple of years beforehand, Bev had got a job on the Channel island of Guernsey, working as a dealer for James Capel, a stockbroking firm, part-owned by HSBC. She had written to Aunty Lena, telling her all about her new life on the island. Lena wrote back saying how nice it was and what a coincidence that our sister Ellen had also done a similar job. Well, this was news to us. What sister Ellen? Bev wrote back straightaway, asking Lena to tell us who this Ellen was. Silence for a while, and then a brief letter saying that she had spoken with Ellen and that Ellen had no desire to meet us. She had her own memories of her Dad and didn't want to hear about ours. Then, realising she had made a major faux-pas, she must have quickly called Mum to tell her what she'd said, clearly having assumed that Bev and I knew of the existence of this half-sister.

I tried going to Mum's sister, Aunty Ethel, for information but was told by her husband Mike that it wasn't fair of me to ask her. Clearly, Bev and I were the only people in the dark. Now Bev, being the more astute of the two of us, told me that it had once dawned on her that there was almost a twenty-year age difference between our parents and that she had actually asked Mum if Dad had ever been married before. 'Yes,' came the short, terse reply. No further explanation was forthcoming. She eventually conceded that Dad and her had decided that Dad would tell us both when we each reached eighteen. Bev had never had such a conversation with Dad, although he allegedly told Mum that he had broached the subject with Bev but that she had said she wasn't interested and didn't want to know anything further. By the time I turned eighteen, he was too far advanced with Alzheimer's for that conversation to ever happen.

We had clearly come up against a brick wall and felt there was nothing more we could do. This was before the era of the internet where answers lay at the click of a mouse. You may well ask why we didn't just ask Mum outright what the truth was, but the reality is she was never what you would call an 'open' person and could get really quite angry when pushed or challenged. Even now, we never get a straight answer to any questions about her and Dad's life together. I think she has forgotten what is fact and what is the version she wants us to believe. There were never any wedding photos in the house nor did they ever celebrate anniversaries, although Mum has always worn a wedding ring on the appropriate finger. I think she feared being vilified as the 'other' woman and getting judged by others and didn't want to bring shame onto her parents. I think she must have always felt a degree of shame and guilt, and those feelings have stuck with her; she still worries about what other people think of her.

Aunty Lena hadn't always been in our lives. Growing up, we had only ever known one grandparent, and that was our maternal grandma who lived with us for a few months in Saughall before her death in March 1976 at the age of seventy-seven. She died of mitral valve stenosis, a common heart problem caused by rheumatic fever in infancy. These days, a relatively straightforward operation would correct this condition. Dad had never talked about his own mother and only ever said that his father had died in the First World War. No siblings were mentioned, and it always seemed a topic that was off limits.

One winter evening in the early 1970s, the telephone rang. Beverley, who was around twelve at the time, answered, and a lady with a Scottish accent asked if it was the right number for Samuel Brunton and if he was there. As she had been taught to do, Bev said, 'Yes, who is speaking please?' to which the reply was 'it's his sister.' Absolutely stunned, she went into the living room to call Dad to come to the phone. We didn't even know he had a sister.

Aunty Lena had been trying to find both Dad and another brother, James, with the help of the Salvation Army but had been unable to locate James. Lena said she hadn't seen James since some time during World War Two when he introduced his girlfriend, Phyllis, who was in the WAAF (Women's Auxiliary Airforce). Nobody in the family had seen or heard from him since then. For some reason, still unknown to us, they had all lost touch, presumably after Dad had left Scotland.

I remember Aunty Lena coming to stay, a tiny, smiling, Scottish lady. Where Dad had dark brown hair and vivid blue eyes, she had fair hair and brown eyes. There were lots of tears and laughter and the sharing of photos. She was actually Dad's half-sister; they shared the same mother but after Dad's father died, his mother went on to remarry and have Lena (short for Helena). The next time it was our turn to visit, and we made the long car journey up to Bathgate near Edinburgh. Bathgate was later put on the map for producing SuBo of Britain's Got Talent fame. I recall how drab all the buildings were. There didn't seem to be any colour anywhere. Aunty Lena and her lovely husband, Uncle Alec, lived in a small end-of-terrace house; their daughter Jo lived like a bookend at the other end of the row. She and her husband Eddie had two children, Karen and Gary. Gary, a year or so older than me, and Karen a bit younger. Aunty Lena had also had a son, Thomas, who was tragically killed in a motorbike accident when he was just twenty-one years old.

It was at Aunty Lena's that I learned how to prepare a real fire in the grate. I still use her technique for rolling newspaper kindling rings, for the open fire in my own bedroom. We made that journey several times over the next few years, spending time wandering around the beautiful city of Edinburgh. On a trip to Glasgow, Mum bought a leather jacket in one of the old warehouses in the Merchant City. Roll on thirty years, and my husband and I now own a gorgeous flat in the Merchant city after the area was gentrified in the late 1990s. What was once the general Post Office is now a block of sumptuous flats with designer shops and fabulous restaurants on the ground floor.

When I was nineteen, my then boyfriend, Alistair, and I went on a driving holiday, travelling up the west coast of Scotland. I rang Aunty Lena to say we would be in the area and would love to call in if it was convenient. It was a bad line as the weather was blowing a storm at the time, but I do recall that she seemed a bit panicked by my call. As it was, it wasn't convenient for her, and so the visit didn't go ahead.

Aunty Lena with Karen and Gary

Mum and Dad with Lena at her house

In 2012, Bev received a message on her http://ancestry.com Family Tree Page from a Robert Brunton. He messaged to say that he had been talking to his grandfather about why he had no family. His grandfather had given Robert his passport and a bit of information and asked him to see what he could find out. Robert had come across our family tree. Robert's grandfather was Dad and Lena's brother, James. Bev messaged back, very excitedly, to say yes, James was our uncle and wouldn't it be fabulous for us all to meet up. Unfortunately, Robert's dad and aunty didn't think that was such a good idea, feeling James was now too old for any new surprises. He was ninety-four at the time. They then made no further effort to maintain any kind of contact. This was a bitter blow, especially as James had clearly given Robert permission to go searching.

James had married Phyllis May in January 1951 in Middlesex, and they went on to have three children: James, born in 1952; Christine, born in 1953; and Stephen, born in 1955. Stephen went on to marry Lorraine Burberry and had a daughter, Anna, in 1980, and a son, Robert, in 1989. Undeterred and feeling we had a right to know, we decided to track down James' whereabouts, and we eventually found him living in New Romney in Kent.

During one school holiday when my own son, Leo, was ten, I decided to go and see if James would talk to me, taking Leo with me for the cute factor. Feeling very nervous, I knocked on the door, which was answered by a sprightly old lady. I babbled out that I was Fiona, Sam's daughter, and Robert had made contact with us, and we'd driven a very long way. It worked; she let us in, but she said only for twenty minutes.Those twenty minutes stretched to over two hours, which Leo recorded on an iPad. It was so lovely to meet James, and I had so many questions. I do have to confess to being very nervous that either Christine or

Stephen would turn up and turf us out, and I did keep listening for a car to pull up. We sat and chatted, often James with a tear of what I imagine was longing in his eyes. Speaking of eyes, I noticed that James had deep brown eyes, unlike Dad whose eyes were vivid blue. Bev has a suspicion regarding Dad's family and their eye colour. She can see no resemblance between the only photo we have of our paternal grandfather and our Dad, and given that Grandma Josephine was seven months pregnant when they married, there is the possibility that Grandfather Samuel was not the biological father to our Dad. Unfortunately, nobody can recall what colour eyes Josephine had, and as brown is the dominant colour, it is odd that Dad was the only Brunton with blue eyes. Without the consent of one of James' children to provide a DNA sample, we will never know for sure if Bev's suspicions are true or not, and sadly, I don't think they would be willing to provide such a sample.

I started by asking James about his memories of Dad, who he said looked like Tyrone Powers, an American actor in the 1930s-1950s, often playing a swashbuckler or playing the romantic leads. I did have to google him, and I can see the similarity! In fact, according to James, Dad was part of an amateur dramatic group himself and regularly took the lead in plays they put on. He also said that for a short time, Dad had played football for the Glasgow Celtic Junior squad before deciding to pursue an academic degree at university. I asked James why it was that he never returned to Glasgow or contacted his family to let them know he was ok. He told me it was because he was ashamed, and that his mother, Granny Brunton, had worked several jobs to be able to afford for him to go to university as he had an aptitude for languages. He said when he failed the first year, he couldn't bring himself to tell her, so he joined the army instead. How utterly tragic is that? At some stage, he must've gone back as I can remember Ellen telling me a story about him going

AWOL (absent without leave), which can mean being dishonourably discharged from the army and at the more extreme end can mean the death penalty if it's in wartime. Apparently, Ellen, who was about seven at the time, was at Granny Brunton's house, and James was asleep in bed when the RMP (Royal Military Police) came knocking on the door looking for him. Quick-thinking Granny bundled him out of the window, quickly putting Ellen in the newly vacated bed so the police wouldn't notice that the empty bed was still warm. This must have been about 1944 when Lena remembers last seeing him. After marrying Phyllis, she and James moved down to the Croydon area before settling in Kent. Phyllis died in 1994, and James went on to marry Daphne, who was the lady who answered the door to us that day.

It was a wonderful two hours that I will forever cherish. I was never to see Uncle James again. He died in May 2014 at ninety-six years of age. Sadly, his children have never been in touch with us and have not responded to any of our attempts to open up communications between us, which is very sad. I only found out he had died by searching through some death registers. After our visit, I sent copies of all the documents and photographs that we had so that they would know about their Dad's family.

Uncle James and his wife with Leo

The only time I ever met him

Aunty Lena's beloved husband, Alec, also died in 1990 of a heart attack whilst mowing the lawn. Sadly, we were unable to attend his funeral, which was disappointing as we were very fond of him. A quietly spoken man with a kind smile and a great sense of humour, like many Scots.

After his death, Lena moved into a flat as she was becoming stiff with arthritis as old age caught up with her. We didn't see her as much, but I always kept in touch by writing her letters.

In 1993, I married Nigel, having met him two years previously in a quirky nightclub in Liverpool called The Cabin. Tucked away on Wood Street, it operated on a membership-only entrance system. That and whether Clive on the door liked the look of you or not! It was a haven for off-duty nurses, police officers, and firemen, of whom Nigel was none, so quite how he got in remains a mystery. Our wedding was a traditional affair, the church service being in Saughall at the church where I had played the Angel Gabrielle in the school nativity performance, aged about six. We even had the same vicar as was there when I was a child, the Reverend Robinson. An unpleasant man for a vicar, to be honest. As a child, he drove a fancy large vintage car that he paraded around the village in, like a character from the To the Manor Born programme on TV. One weekend, there was the annual Rose Queen fete where decorated floats would drive through the village, Reverend Robinson leading the way in his posh car. As the parade came down our road, The Ridings, steam began to billow out of his engine. He stopped the car outside our house and foolishly opened the car bonnet, immediately releasing hot steam directly into his face. If it hadn't been for Mum's quick thinking and medical intervention, he may well have been scarred for life. He didn't ever acknowledge what she did for him.

After the wedding service, Mum surprised us by having the Chester Town Cryer appear outside the church, reading from a scroll, announcing our marriage. On the wedding video, Reverend Robinson can be heard shouting, 'It's not a village, it's a hamlet,' before slamming the vestry door shut. Pompous old fool!

The following year, our daughter, Abigail, was born, and less than two years later, twins, Sam and Ben. I had always wanted to name any son I had Sam, after Dad, believing I was the last in the family line to carry the surname Brunton. I even kept my maiden name, as did Bev, after getting married.

A year after Abbie was born, Nigel got offered a job working as Fund Manager in the Japanese markets in London. So, in 1995 we left the Chester area and moved to Berkhamsted in Hertfordshire. I found a job as a part-time nurse, and Nigel became a commuter! Almost seven years later, we had a little surprise, and Leo arrived. We were now a family of six plus Rafferty, the Tibetan Terrier.

In 2004, less than a year after Leo was born, we moved to San Francisco in California, where we spent the next four years living the 'American Dream'. Several years later, during a visit from Nigel's parents one Christmas, we realised the dream was likely over. My father-in-law, Bernard, suffered a TIA, a heart attack essentially, the night they arrived. After a short but expensive hospital stay, he was released from the hospital with the advice not to do any more long-distance flights. Coupled with the fact that Abbie was due to start high school, and so if we were going to leave, now was the time, we decided to return to the UK.

Not wanting to return to the village of Potten End in Hertfordshire as it would mean sending the three older kids to a school that had bombed its Ofsted Report several times running, we had to choose where to move to. Now, I don't advocate making huge decisions the way we made this one. We sat around the kitchen, with a bottle of wine and a map of Britain plus a pin. I knew I didn't want to live south of London as this would add an extra hour onto my drive up to Chester any time I wanted to visit Mum. We had to be somewhere that was going to be a reasonable commute time for Nigel into London. So, we closed our eyes and stuck the pin on the map. It stuck on a place called Cookham in Berkshire. The decision was made; we were going to move there. I went online and eventually found a house to rent, went online again, and rented furniture to go in the rented house. We landed at Heathrow on a very wet, miserable day in July. The kids were not impressed. We arrived, via satnav, at our new home in Cookham only to find we didn't fit in it. It was tiny.

A few weeks later, our forty-foot container arrived with everything we owned in it and was promptly put into storage. We had a six-month lease on the house, so I was on a mission to find us a home to buy very soon.

Three years later, in 2010, Abbie and I travelled up to Edinburgh with Bev to visit (pre-arranged) Aunty Lena. It was a lovely afternoon spent talking about Dad over cups of tea and slices of cake. This was probably the last time we saw Aunty Lena as shortly afterwards, in 2011, she died at the age of eighty-seven years. I only found out she had died when her daughter, Jo, left a message with my young son letting me know. By the time she had called me, Aunty Lena had already been buried; another funeral we were unable to attend.

Abbie, Aunty Lena and me

The last time I saw Aunty Lena before she died

CHAPTER 4: THE SEARCH FOR THE TRUTH

By 2011, the World Wide Web had well and truly arrived, and information was a mere click away. Following the death of Aunty Lena, Bev and I realised that we were rapidly running out of time if we ever hoped to find this missing sister, Ellen, and we were also very concerned that, given the age difference, she might not even still be alive and we would lose the chance forever.

Bev became the internet sleuth and set about finding the truth. Following a fall down the stairs, she'd had to have an operation and was off work and unable to drive for eight weeks. All of a sudden, she had time on her hands, lots of it. She had tried the odd search in the past, but we knew only four basic facts, and searching under Samuel Brunton, born in Canada, on the 14th of July 1915 had previously given zilch returns. We didn't even know our paternal grandmother's name! All we had was:

1) Dad was born in Canada.

2) His father had died during the First World War (we assumed killed in action).

3) His mother had remarried, and his stepfather had died in an asylum.

4) He'd been married before and had a daughter called Ellen.

New records were being added all the time, and so starting with a free trial on Ancestry.com, Bev tried again, and on this occasion, she got a hit. Ships' records had since been digitised and uploaded to the website, and there he was, on the ship The Saturnia, travelling with his mother and younger brother, James, then aged eight months, from Canada to Scotland. Finally, we had our grandmother's name, Josephine. Immediately Ancestry hints came up with a wedding record in Canada that matched. We then had her maiden name (Gourlay), the names of her parents (Sarah McSefferney and James Gourlay), plus our grandfather's name, Samuel, and his parents (Samuel Branigan and Mary McKinnon). Here was a huge obstacle we had come across previously when trying to do searches: the family line using the surname Brunton seemed to disappear once we got past our grandfather. We ended up paying a genealogist to do some research for us, and she discovered that our great-grandfather, then living in America, had, for some reason, changed his surname from Branigan to Brunton. Just why he did that we will never know, but back then, it wasn't illegal to do it.

Bev began to build a family tree, spending hours on Ancestry, Scotland's census websites, ordering birth, marriage, and death certificates galore. All to no avail. So then she tried searching in England, and bingo, there it was. Dad had married Catherine (Katie) Shevlin on the nineteenth of April, 1938, in Tottenham, London. The next step was to look for any children from that marriage. It became evident that Ellen was not the only half-sister we had. There appeared to be five half-siblings we never knew existed. Two girls and three boys. How could no one have told us? Why did no one tell us? We didn't dare, at that time, to confront Mum with what we had found out. It was all really quite overwhelming but equally very exciting.

It has subsequently become clear that everyone else in our family knew the truth. I realised this later when I posted some photos on social media of us, with our half-siblings, and not one of our relatives questioned who these 'new' siblings were. I find it really difficult to accept that the only two blood relatives to these half siblings are the only two people to have been kept in the dark about their existence. That is just not right, nor is it fair.

We set about trying to locate them all. Using the power of the web, Bev slowly uncovered them all, and they all lived in Scotland. It was all quite tricky as Scotland has different laws regarding access to official records. At one point, Bev and I headed back up to Edinburgh to visit the ScotlandsPeople Office in a bid to try and find more records. We ended up finding, to our immense shock, another half-brother, David, born in 1949.

Eventually, we had a list of potential names and addresses for them all. We decided that I would write to all the Ellens on the list. I think that was the most scared I've ever felt, writing those letters. Bev admits to losing her bottle at this stage: knowing we had found them in principle was one thing, but taking the next step seemed a massive move. She felt there was a huge potential for us to be rejected and possibly causing a lot of hurt. But equally, like me, she had an immense desire to reach out.

The wait for a reply was agonising. I received a very curt letter from one Ellen Lang that said she definitely wasn't our sister and could we kindly not contact her again. We hastily scribbled her name off the list.

I was actually looking for paint in Homebase when the reply finally came, some three weeks later.

My mobile phone rang, and a tentative voice at the other end said, "Hello, Fiona, my name is Ellen, and I think I'm your sister."

I spent the next three hours sitting on the bed display of the store talking to her. There were so many questions I didn't know where to start. What was evident was that she had no idea of our existence either. Lena had clearly lied to us all those years ago when she said Ellen didn't want to have any contact. She told me that after receiving my letter, she had sat on it for three weeks trying to decide if she wanted to open up her heart to any possible further pain. Dad had walked out on her when she was just fourteen years old.

After three hours, my phone was about to die, so I arranged to call her back from the landline once I got home. Firstly though, I had to tell Bev. I called her number and told her to pour herself a stiff drink and to sit down, and then I told her all that I had talked about with Ellen.

Over the coming days, so many phone conversations were had as we spoke to some of our 'new' siblings. I had a huge notepad and pen by the phone as I tried to get a handle on who had which children.

The conversation that still makes me laugh was the one I had with Peter, the fourth child who is known as Big Pedro. Bearing in mind they all had very broad Glaswegian accents, I often only caught every third word they were saying. I was clearly out of practice; Dad had been gone such a long time I was no longer used to hearing the accent. Our first conversation went like this:

'Hello, aye, I'm Peter, or big Pedro.'

'Hello, erm, Peter, it's really lovely to finally speak to you. Are you married?'

'Aye, to Ann.'

'Great, do you have kids?'

'Aye, we've got big Peter, Ross, Angela and wee Peter.'

'Hi, yes, sorry, I've just written down that you have three sons and two of them are called Peter?'

'Aye, that's right.'

No explanation, nothing. Further down the line we were to learn that Big Pedro had had a relationship that resulted in a baby boy being adopted by another family. Years later, when he and Ann were married and had children together, they named their son Peter after his father. Roll on sixteen years and that adopted son comes looking for his birth father, and by sheer coincidence, his adoptive parents had called him Peter.

If that wasn't confusing enough, there are a lot of Sams within the family. I need not have worried about calling my son Sam nor worried that the name Brunton was going to die out with me; there are loads of them, I'm very happy to say! Equally, there are two other sets of non-identical twins in the family, as well as my own pair, Sam and Ben! So many Sams and Peters.

Peter wearing the self-designed Brunton tartan

Ellen on her wedding day

So, Ellen was born a month before her parents married, in March 1938, in London. She is only five years younger than mine and Bev's mum. The following year, as war broke out, they moved back to Glasgow, assuming it was safer to be there. I imagine the move was also to be closer to family. Two years later, in 1940, a second daughter arrived, Josephine, named after Dad's mum. The family was living in the Baillieston area of Glasgow. Dad, by this time, was working as an electrical welder on the ships in John Brown's Shipyards on the River Clyde, and Katie was at home with the children.

In 1942, their first son, Sam, was born, followed three years later by Peter and another son, Edward, in 1948, and finally, David, born in 1949.

Sadly, by the time we found them, David, the youngest half-sibling, had died of cancer in 2010. My youngest son, Leo, is the spitting image of David as a child. So much so that I showed Leo's friends a black-and-white photo of David, and they all thought it was Leo.

CHAPTER 5: FINALLY MEETING

We had still not said anything at all to Mum at this stage. We booked into a hotel on the outskirts of Glasgow. Peter and Ann were going to come and pick us up, and we were all to drive to Ellen's house, a short distance away. To say we were nervous would be putting it mildly. Bev and I stood outside the hotel, looking for Peter's car to pull up. My palms were sweating, and Bev was chain smoking in the car park! Eventually, we saw his car pull in. I was hiding behind a pillar as I had completely lost my bottle with Bev doing her nut, saying, 'Don't you dare leave me now, this was your idea,' and dragging me out before they could see me.

When I looked up, Dad was walking towards us, only it wasn't Dad, I knew it wasn't, but my God, the man walking towards us was the image of him. It made me feel very emotional. It's an indescribable feeling when you meet someone that you're related to and yet have never known, for the first time. I've watched the show, 'Long Lost Family,' many times (been there, got the t-shirt), and have often heard others say that there is a feeling of instant connection, of knowing, of shared blood, I guess. That is exactly how it felt meeting Peter and Ellen that day. A feeling of completeness, of the circle being rounded.

The two of us got in the back of Peter's car where we said hello to Ann, Peter's wife, who was sitting in the driver's seat, and we set off to Ellen's house. I can honestly say that was one of the funniest car journeys I have ever made. It quickly became clear that neither Peter nor Ann had any sense of direction whatsoever. Bev and I could hear a satnav giving directions but couldn't actually see one on show.

They had carefully programmed it before setting off, and then Peter decided to steadfastly ignore it, putting it in the glove box, as soon as they set off, leaving it to issue directions in utter vain. Now, Ellen only lived about five miles from the hotel, so after forty minutes of Bev and I nudging each other and trying not to giggle on the back seat, I asked if Ellen had recently moved to the area, therefore assuming Peter had not actually visited Ellen in this house. No, Ellen had been at this particular address for several years, and Peter had visited her there on many occasions, Ann who had, by now, lost the will to live, was approaching a roundabout when Peter shouted, 'Follow that car, I know that man.' Bev and I were creased up laughing by this point.

Forty-five minutes later, having driven past Strathclyde Country Park at least three times, we finally pulled up outside Ellen's house. I remember the door opening, Peter going in first, followed by Bev, and thinking this is it, in five seconds I'll see the face of the sister we've waited decades to meet.

Recognising your own mannerisms in a stranger is a very weird feeling. The more we looked, the more similarities we could all see in each other. I was still taken aback by just how like Dad Peter looked.

We had gone laden with photographs. I had tried to be diplomatic and had not taken any photos of Mum and Dad together. I don't know why I worried; they brought out lots of photos of Dad and Catherine (Katie) together. It felt a little strange seeing Dad's handsome smiling face next to that of his wife who wasn't our Mum. What became evident very early on, and what has caused a great deal of hurt, is the fact that Aunty Lena clearly knew both sides of the family and yet didn't let one side know about the other. I do wonder if she felt bitter about the fact that despite Josephine remarrying after Grandad Samuel died, she was still always known as Granny Brunton and not Granny Brownlie after her own father, and that Josephine spent the rest of her life supporting Katie and our Dad's children.

Ellen had been very close to her Aunty Lena and both her and Sam felt her betrayal the hardest. For Bev and I, we finally understood why we were not told about either Lena's death or Uncle Alec's until after they were both buried. Their son, Dougie, was Peter's best friend. We didn't even know that Dougie existed. I'm not sure how cousin Jo, Lena's daughter, kept us a secret from him for all that time. Especially how she managed to get Gary and Karen to keep the family secret. My own kids would've been rubbish.

Ellen had married the love of her life, another Peter. Her mum, Katie, hadn't approved of the relationship and so had arranged for Ellen to go and stay with one of her sisters in New York in the hope that the romance would cool off. As she was underage to travel overseas alone without the consent of both parents, a solicitor had contacted Dad requesting his written permission for Ellen to travel. The separation failed to succeed in splitting them up, and Ellen returned to Scotland and back into the arms of Peter. The two of them married and had five children together: Donald, Sheena, Morag, Graham, and David. Both Sheena and Morag lived in the south of England, not far from me at all. In fact, at one point, Sheena was living near Berkhamsted, her son attending a school in the town, and we lived in the neighbouring village of Potten End. It is perfectly feasible to think we may well have passed each other on the High Street or that our sons could have played on the same football team. These days, Morag and her family live about forty-five minutes from our home in the home counties, and half-brother Sam's daughter, Roslyn, lives less than an hour away from us too.

There are so many occasions where we could've accidentally met or that I could have walked past one of our siblings whilst at our flat in Glasgow.

Peter and Ann

We were so excited to meet them. We were picking them up at a hotel near Baillieston, which used to be Glasgow zoo. We arrived at the car park, and I remember feeling very nervous, excited, and apprehensive about what was ahead of us. I thought these two women might be people I don't want in my life, and yet they are our family.

When I met them, my fears vanished as the first hugs were so warm and sincere that it just melted my heart. I just knew I would always be in their lives and I welcomed them into mine. I was struck by the resemblance to their Glasgow family. There was no doubt that they were Brunton stock!

I'd also thought the conversation might be a little awkward, but it just flowed really well. I was driving, and Peter was navigating as this was his territory, so I trusted his instructions. We reached a roundabout, and Peter said, 'follow that car' without stating which one. So that started the journey of taking the long road instead of the shortcut. We were having our usual banter, but it must have sounded unbelievable to Bev and Fi, and I could see them in my mirror giggling in the back seat, unsure of what to say, having only met fifteen minutes prior! We eventually arrived at Ellen's house and had a fabulous time getting to know one another. Such a good vibe and very relaxing. I love my sister-in-laws!

The following day, we drove to the Glasgow Infirmary where Sam was an inpatient. He had been treated for bowel cancer and had recently had further surgery. We walked onto the ward and were directed to a four-bed bay. I didn't need the nurse to tell me which of the four men in the room was our half-brother. Here again was a man who looked just like Dad. So much so that Bev walked straight off the ward again in order to compose herself. It was such a shock seeing Sam like that; it brought back memories of Dad in a hospital bed in his final weeks, and she found herself almost completely overwhelmed and very tearful. That was another very emotional meeting, Sam looking disbelievingly at photos of Dad and Lena together at Lena's house in Bathgate. I honestly think that if it were not for those photographs, he would not have believed us when we told him that Lena had been in touch with his Dad for over thirty years. That must have really hurt.

Sam was fondly known as 'The Prof' amongst his family. A quiet, intelligent man who spent all his working life as a librarian and was a very popular and respected figure within his local community. He married his childhood sweetheart, May, and they went on to have three children: Roslyn, Duncan, and Samantha. In 1967 (the year I was born), they emigrated to Ontario, Canada where Sam did a master's degree and continued to work locally as a librarian. Whilst there, he composed a book called 'Sketches and History of Parry Sound', which is still in circulation today. Sam and May moved back to Scotland in 1973, settling back into life in Glasgow.

The next time we saw Sam was at his home where we got to meet Samantha, his youngest daughter, and her two children, Kerr and Robyn, who lived a few doors away. By now, Sam was becoming increasingly unwell and was clearly very weak. He died a short time later in 2014. Bev and I are so grateful that we did get to meet him. He was such a kind soul. We were both overwhelmed and felt privileged to be asked to attend his funeral and even got acknowledged as Sam's sisters by the priest during the service. It was at his funeral that I saw cousin Jo, Aunty Lena's daughter, for the first time since I was a child. She was there with her husband, Eddie, and her brother, Dougie, who must have wondered who on earth we were. I could see a flicker of recognition when she saw me quickly followed by surprise. That was the first time Bev had met her. Unfortunately, we didn't get a chance to talk as they left straight after the funeral service.

In December of the same year, at the age of seventy-six, we lost the funny, vivacious Ellen too. We did get to meet her a few more times over the years, mainly whilst she was an inpatient in the hospital. She'd had a chronic illness for a few years, it finally getting the better of her. She kept her sense of humour to the very end and still raised a smile when she saw you. We just so wish that we had found them sooner.

The next half-sibling for us to meet was Edward, who also lived in Glasgow. We met him at Peter and Ann's house one Sunday morning. Physically, he was not as similar to Dad as Sam and Peter were, but he had so many of Dad's mannerisms. Charming, flamboyant and, like Dad, talked with his hands. He was very creative and attended the Glasgow School of Art in his youth. Edward had never married but had a beautiful daughter, Elizabeth, who had her dad's creative flair.

Sadly, but perfectly understandably, Dad's second-born daughter, Josephine, has chosen not to meet Bev and I. We do hope that in time, she will change her mind. In the meantime, we have to accept her decision. What has amazed both Bev and I is the warmth and generosity that these new siblings have shown us, that they knew absolutely nothing of us, have no reason to share any part of themselves with us, and yet have welcomed us into their lives as if we were all raised together under one roof. We fully appreciate that for some it doesn't always work out this way; we are incredibly lucky and grateful.

Here is an article I found written about Sam by Ian Bunting:

Sad loss as former long-serving Coatbridge College librarian dies

Tributes have been paid to a much-loved Coatbridge librarian after he lost his lengthy battle with illness.

Sam Brunton, who worked at Coatbridge College for over 30 years, passed away on Monday at the age of 71, just five months before he was due to celebrate his golden wedding anniversary to his beloved wife May.

Shawhead man Sam worked in the college library for 31 years — from 1974 until his retirement in 2005.

He also played a huge role in the development of activities for youngsters in his community.

Along with other Shawhead residents, Sam established the village's first youth club in St Bernard's Church.

The club proved so popular it expanded to Shawhead Community Centre and Sam helped to organise trips abroad.

Selfless Sam also worked as a volunteer with the Coatbridge branch of the St Andrew's Ambulance Association, eventually becoming Commandant.

Daughter Samantha Downie, 37, paid tribute to her beloved dad: "My dad was a really lovely man and hugely enjoyed getting involved in the community. He was also involved in the running of under-14 football for local youngsters and made a real impression on people of all ages.

"Many Coatbridge residents still have fond memories of the times spent at the youth club in Shawhead and the trips they went on, most memorably a visit to Coatbridge's twin town of St Denis in France.

"He will be very sadly missed by the whole family and everyone who knew him."

Coatbridge MP Tom Clarke also paid tribute to Sam: "I am so sorry to hear of Sam's passing.

"He was well known in Coatbridge and the wider community, well respected and highly regarded and my thoughts are with his family at this sad time."

Sam leaves behind wife May, son Duncan, daughters Roslyn and Samantha and seven grandchildren.

His funeral will take place at St Bernard's Church in Shawhead this Saturday at 10am.[1]

---

[1] Daily Record. (2014). *Sad loss of former long-serving Coatbridge politician Tom Nolan*. [online] Available at: https://www.dailyrecord.co.uk/news/local-news/sad-loss-former-long-serving-coatbridge-3486167 [Accessed 14 Aug. 2024].

CHAPTER 6: BACK TO THE BEGINNING

We've always known that Dad was born in Hamilton, a small industrial town outside of Toronto, Canada. We knew that he arrived in Glasgow via a ship, The Saturnia, along with his mother and baby brother, James, when he was four years old. What we didn't know was why. Bev became a keyboard warrior once again.

Our paternal grandmother was called Josephine Gourlay, and she was born on 19 December 1894 in Old Cumnock in the county of Ayr. On her birth certificate, her own mother is clearly illiterate and has signed the parish register with an 'X' by her name. Her father, James Gourlay, was a coal miner, as were all his relations. It must have been like jumping from the frying pan into the fire to some extent as her own grandparents originated from Ireland and had fled to Scotland during the seven-year Irish Potato famine in 1845. Josephine was the last one of fourteen children.

It would have been a life spent in poverty. They lived in a row of houses called Miners' Rows. Living conditions were so bad that a report was commissioned, which resulted in these houses being pulled down. There were often up to fourteen people living in two rooms and open sewage toilets that were shared between many houses. The miners at this time could only buy food and essential supplies from shops owned by the mine owners, as were their homes. In some cases, the miners, instead of receiving a pay packet, would be given food coupons instead. If there were complaints or dissent, it often resulted in entire families being evicted and thrown out onto the streets.

These evictions became famous and became subject to government enquiries, leading to a massive change in legislation. Both the McSefferneys and the Gourlays were known as Ayrshire miners, and conditions for them were particularly bad.

In the year 1894, when Josephine was born, The National Union of Scottish Mineworkers was founded. It was set up to improve working conditions and pay for the miners, the union often voting to strike to get their message heard. Life was hard; the average life expectancy for a man was forty-nine years. When they weren't striking, mining did provide employment and a steady income. Schooling at that time was limited to the better-off, so it was common for sons to follow their fathers down the mines to help support the family. I would think many of Josephine's eight brothers did just that.

At the turn of the seventeenth century, the British Empire was expanding and emigration became easier with the establishment of the Virginia Company led by Captain John Smith. The Empire needed people with specific skill sets, much like Australia still does today. Getting to Canada by sea back then would take two weeks and many passengers died en route, having contracted dysentery and smallpox which spread rapidly in the cramped and overcrowded conditions on board.

In May of 1913, at twenty years of age, Josephine decided to head to Canada to start a new life and boarded the ship 'The Hesperian', sailing from Glasgow to Canada. According to the ship's records, she was going to work in domestic service in Toronto. Next to her name on the ship's purser's list, it says 'British Bonus Allowed'. This was a commission paid by the Canadian government's Immigration Branch to steamship booking agents in the UK and in European countries for each suitable immigrant who purchased a ticket to sail to Canada. This was at a time when Canada was looking for people to emigrate there to grow the population. The Hesperian was later torpedoed on 4 September 1915 by U20, commanded by Cdr W. von Schwieger. There were thirty-two fatalities as a direct result and the ship sank.

There is a lot of misinformation from around this time. Ellen had been led to believe that Josephine ran away to New York at sixteen years old with a slightly older friend and that the two of them boarded a ship from Southampton and arrived at Ellis Island, where all passengers were processed prior to being allowed to enter the United States. Josephine had also claimed to be eighteen years old on arrival and had supposedly later found work as a nanny. It was believed that her distraught parents sent two of her brothers to New York to bring her back home. I found this not to be the case after researching the passenger database for all immigrants that entered New York via Ellis Island and there is no record of a Josephine Gourlay having ever arrived, via boat, in the United States nor could I find any evidence of any of her eight brothers having entered America either.

Many Scots emigrated to Canada; in fact, many of the streets in Toronto are named the same as those in Glasgow and Edinburgh, such as Dundas Street. They began arriving as early as the seventeenth century and by 1870, there were over 170,000 Scots settled there, notably in the Quebec and Ontario provinces.

At some point, and we don't know where or when, she met our grandfather, Samuel Brunton. Samuel was also born in Glasgow in April 1889 but emigrated to Canada in 1890 with several members of his family and appears on a

New York census aged nine months old as a US citizen. No records can be found as to how the family entered the USA from Canada, but we could see that Samuel's own father did not move with them; he remained in Kingston until his death in 1905. We have to assume the marriage broke down and they separated. Years later, our grandfather's army attestation papers state that he had not had contact with his father for twenty-eight years. Also on that census is Ann Rintoul, his grandmother; her daughter, Mary (our great grandmother); an older brother, Alexander; and his father, Samuel. Another census in 1891 revealed that Ann Rintoul was then living in the city of Kingston in the county of Frontenac in Ontario. Also living with her was a Mary Brunton linked to a Samuel Branigan. In the 1910 census Grandfather Samuel was back living in New York and was listed as an Umbrella Maker and living with his mother, Mary. Had I known all of this when we moved to the States ourselves in 2004 it could have saved us a lot of stress and saved us applying for a visa.

Samuel and Josephine were married on 26 May 1915 in Toronto, him stating he was a salesman and that they were both Presbyterian, which is interesting as on the ship's records Josephine states she was a Roman Catholic. None of their respective families attended the wedding, which was witnessed by neighbours, Walter White and his wife, who lived at 5 Tacoma Avenue, Hamilton. On the marriage certificate, Samuel was twenty-six years old and Josephine twenty-three years old. Less than two months later, on 14 July 1915, Josephine gave birth to twins, Sam (our Dad) and Margaret. She was actually only twenty-one at the time, and World War I had been raging for almost a year. By now they were living in a small town called Hamilton, thirty-five miles from Toronto and fifty-five miles southeast of New York. The town lies at the extreme western end of Lake Ontario and was first settled in 1815. It has a port on one side and an escarpment on the other that locals refer to as 'the Mountain'. When Samuel and Josephine were there, it was an industrial town known for its port and rail connections. Even today it is one of Canada's leading industrial centres, being well known for its iron and steel industry.

The newly married couple lived at 4 Tacoma Avenue, a smart, three-storey end-of-terrace house in a small cul-de-sac. It's unclear if they had the whole house or if they rented a room or flat within the property. When the twins were seventeen months old, tragedy struck and Margaret died. The death certificate states the cause of death as influenza, but it is quite possible she had Spanish flu, which was rampant in Canada at that time. She is buried in an unmarked grave in Mount Pleasant cemetery in Toronto. When Nigel and I visited Toronto, a very kind groundsman paced out where she lay by the plot number we gave him, in an area reserved for the graves of babies and children. It was so sad to know she had lain there for nearly a hundred years without any kind of memorial stone. I had bought a small plaque and a Scottish flag and taken them to Canada with us. I'm so glad we did, as these are now the only signs of anyone having ever visited her grave site. Dad had always believed his twin died after choking on a banana.

Samuel senior joined the war effort, having signed up to the Canadian Overseas Expeditionary Force on 20 April 1917. He stated his skill as being that of a carpenter, although he had stated on his wedding certificate he was a salesman. His attestation paper shows that he had previously served as a private in the US army and had been rejected by the Royal Canadian Navy Volunteer Reserve due to poor eyesight, but Bev believes this is unlikely as in the only photograph we have of him, he is not wearing any glasses. It is more likely that he already had tuberculosis at this time and that is why he was rejected. He had clearly been keen to serve his country, trying every avenue possible to get in on the war effort. He eventually got his wish and became a private with the seventh Forestry Battalion before being promoted to sergeant after six months. His records state that he was 'of good character,' which would explain the quick promotion.

Sadly, a year later, tragedy struck again. Samuel had tuberculosis and was admitted to the sanatorium up on the 'mountain' in Hamilton, known locally as The San, which had only opened in 1906 with just four patients. It was believed in those days that the best treatment for tuberculosis was fresh air, so these sanatoriums were built so that each ward had a veranda on which the patients could be wheeled out, on their beds, to breathe the fresh mountain air. The sanatorium still exists today, but is now called the Chedoke Hospital. After the Second World War, hundreds of indigenous people from the north of Canada were treated for tuberculosis at the sanatorium, and there remains a small museum of some of their artwork on display there. In 2013, we travelled to Toronto to follow the trail of Josephine and Samuel and got to visit the hospital while there. There is a large memorial stone in the grounds to commemorate all those who died there during the First World War.

Half-brother Sam had a letter that Grandfather Samuel had written to Josephine while he was an inpatient. He starts the letter with 'Dear Wife', and goes on to request that she bring him his suit, gloves, boots, and hat brush. Quite what he thought he would need any of these for while an inpatient, I can't imagine. It reads very formally and more than a little bit pompous, with no hint of affection, nor does he ask about the welfare of his son Sam or of her impending birth (James). It's quite possible the letter was dictated to a volunteer or hospital staff member, which could explain the formality of the letter. I hope that is the reason for its apparent coldness.

The Sanatorium in Hamilton, Canada where our grandfather, Samuel, died

The memorial cairn outside the Sanatorium that is now The Chedoke Hospital, dedicated to all those that died at the hospital in the First World War

My son, Sam Brunton, next to the War Grave of his Great Grandfather

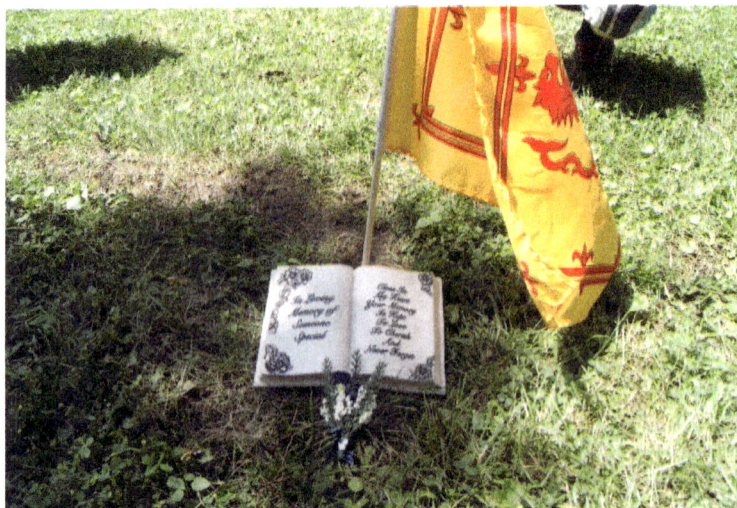

The unmarked grave of Dad's twin, Margaret

At just twenty-nine years of age, Samuel succumbed to tuberculosis on 25 November 1918 at the sanatorium. It was only eleven days after the First World War ended. His young widow, Josephine, gave birth to their second son, James, just five days later. Within one year, she had lost a child and then her husband and was alone with a toddler and a newborn to provide for and care for. She must have been devastated and had no family around to help her.

It's hardly surprising then that she made the decision to return to Glasgow in Scotland to have the support of her family. They set sail from Montreal on 15 July 1919, a day after Sam turned four years old, on the steamship Saturnia, part of the Cunard Line. According to the ship's records, she was a twenty-seven-year-old housewife travelling with a four-year-old son and baby James, who is now eight months old. Josephine was, in fact, only twenty-five years of age. At some point on the two-week journey, she had a professional photograph taken of her, our Dad, and baby James.

Josephine with four-year-old (Sam) and baby James on the ship returning to Glasgow.

Grandfather Samuel

They arrived back in the port of Glasgow, and the three of them went to live with Josephine's mother, Sarah Gourlay, at 36 Ann Terrace in Bo'ness. One of the reasons why Josephine was persuaded to come home was that her mother was thought to be very poorly. However, it was another ten years before Great Grandma Sarah died, in June 1929, of complications of heart failure. Josephine's brother, William, had been living with Sarah since 1911. He never married but appears to have cared for not only his brothers and sisters but also his nephews and nieces. It was William who notified Sarah's death on the death certificate.

It is thought that when she left Canada, Josephine had hopes of one day being able to return and so had all of her furniture put in storage, which ended up being sold some twenty-five years later for a considerable amount of money. I suspect this wasn't the case as both she and Samuel were both very young to have acquired expensive furniture, and they were only together for four years and living off his army wages. The fact that they could not afford a headstone for baby Margaret's grave suggests that they were not affluent by any means. I do recall Aunty Lena telling Bev and I that Josephine had indeed bought a passage back to Canada and had been planning on leaving Sam and James to care for her (Lena). This was after the death of her second husband, Thomas Brownlie and that she was only stopped when one of her sisters threatened to call the police if she went ahead and left them. I hope that story isn't true; from all that we have learned about Josephine, it seems unlikely that this was the case.

There would have been a very real fear for Josephine that if she could not afford to care for the boys, then they could have all ended up in the Poor House. The Glasgow Poor House was located on what is now Hanover Street and

67

opened in 1809. It was originally built as an insane asylum and was one of the largest in the UK.

Conditions inside were pretty grim with poor sanitation, poor lighting, and poor ventilation. A perfect breeding ground for all sorts of diseases, not somewhere you would have wanted for yourself or for your children. The poor law system was only abolished in 1948 after the introduction of the National Assistance Act. This Act put the responsibility for the welfare of the poor in the hands of local authorities.

At this time, there was a shortage of men too; approximately 70,000 Scottish soldiers died in the First World War, and this had a huge impact on Scotland's economy and industrial production. The average age for a British soldier in 1914 was thirty years old, and as high as fifty-one years of age. With this in mind, it was hardly surprising that in 1920, Josephine accepted a marriage proposal from a Mr Thomas Brownlie, a thirty-year-old tobacconist from Bo'ness. Thomas had also been a soldier and had been stationed out in Egypt. He was also divorced and had three children, Agnes, aged ten, Mary, aged nine, and son, Andrew, aged seven years old. Whilst in Egypt, he received word from his father that his wife, Marion, had been having an affair. Thomas sent word back home for his father to begin divorce proceedings against Marion on his behalf. The two daughters were put in Quarrier's Home Orphanage in Bridge of Weir, and young Andrew, known as Mac, was taken in by his paternal grandparents to live in Lochleven road in Glasgow. Court records state that Marion could be heard banging on the court doors demanding to speak to the judge in a desperate bid to get her children back. Her attempts were futile; the only contact she would have with them over the next few years was via the Salvation Army, who kept in regular contact with the orphanage and Marion.

It was at the Salvation Army that Marion met William Ogilvie, who helped her get visiting rights to see the girls. She later went on to marry William, and they had five children together: Isabell, John, Morag, May, and Robert. Their grandson, Stuart, has happy memories of staying with his grandparents in their two-room apartment where, he says, there was a bed in the kitchen wall that he said was fun to sleep in.

Thomas Brownlie and Josephine were married on 13th March 1920 in Glasgow and moved to Star Place in Bo'ness, where Thomas became a sub postmaster. Josephine was now the mother to Sam and James and the stepmother to seven-year-old Mac. Dad recalled this as a deeply unhappy time in his life, as Thomas was a cruel man and regularly beat him and James with a leather belt. He also forced Josephine to denounce her first marriage to Samuel, the boys' father, in a church. Thomas was a Roman Catholic and so wanted to be wed in a church. Because Samuel had been a Presbyterian, the Catholic church did not 'recognise' that marriage. Thomas was, in fact, making Sam and James 'bastards' in the eyes of the Church. Seeing his mother deny her marriage to his beloved father had a profound effect on Dad, and he harboured a hatred of churches thereafter. In fact, when he was in the midst of Alzheimer's, if we ever attended a church ceremony of any kind, we would have to cover the church noticeboard in order to get him to go inside. He was also adamant that I was not to be christened into any religion. A belief that I myself have, and as such, none of my own children are christened either. Faith to me is a life choice, not something that is forced upon an uninformed child.

Two years later, in 1922, Josephine gave birth to a daughter, Sarah, who was born prematurely and died just eight short hours later. Another daughter arrived in 1924, and this one was healthy; Aunty Lena had arrived.

The following year, Thomas became ill and was admitted to Bellsdyke Hospital, also known as Larbert lunatic asylum, in Falkirk. Dad told me that as a child, he and Josephine would have to get two buses a day to the asylum to feed Thomas, as food was not provided for the patients. Thomas died in the asylum on 3rd January 1926. Dad was under the impression that he died as a result of a brain injury caused by shrapnel from the First World War. What Thomas's death certificate actually states as the cause of death was Dementia Paralytica. 'A disease of the central nervous system characterised by mental deterioration, speech defects, and progressive paralysis.'

In other words, Syphilis, presumably contracted in Egypt during the war. Rather ironic, given that he divorced his first wife, Marion, for alleged infidelity.

CHAPTER 7: WIDOWED LIFE

Once again, Josephine found herself widowed. By now, she was thirty-three years old and had lost two husbands and two infants. With Thomas gone, she got Agnes and Mary out of the orphanage, and, along with Mac, they were reunited with their mother Marion and William. Daughter Mary married George Townsend in Galashiels, living there until her death in 1977. Agnes, known as Nancy, went on to become a nurse and later emigrated, in 1964, to Australia, living to the ripe old age of one hundred. Young Mac went on to join the RAF as an aircraft fitter but was tragically killed flying back from Egypt, in what was one of the worst air crashes of the Second World War, on 16 March 1942. The plane crashed into a hillside in Ireland, killing fourteen young men but leaving one survivor. Mac was just twenty-nine years old, single, and had no children. He is buried in Sighthill cemetery in Glasgow. Peter, Abbie, Leo, and I were able to attend a ceremony there as a new headstone was finally put in place (after sixty-two years of there not being one) by the Commonwealth War Graves Commission, for him, in 2016. The original headstone had been removed in 1954 after the ground at the cemetery was deemed 'unsafe'. Here is an article about this particular instance written by Lynn McPherson:

Mac (Top Right)

World War Two hero to have headstone replaced after 62 years in unmarked grave

ANDREW Brownlie's headstone was removed in 1954 due to safety fears, but now the marker is being replaced as part of the Commonwealth War Graves Commission.

A WORLD War II airman will this week have his grave marked for the first time in 62 years.

RAF fitter Andrew Brownlie's headstone was removed in 1954 after ground at Glasgow's Sighthill Cemetery was declared unsafe.

Now the Commonwealth War Graves Commission are restoring Andrew's grave, along with 83 others, in a ceremony next week.

His great-niece Fiona Barrett is travelling from her Maidstone home to be there.

She said: "When I looked into our family tree and finally traced him, we found him in an unmarked grave.

"The CWGC were brilliant. They said he was on a list for a new headstone.

"Eventually I got a call to say there would be a - ceremony. I felt I had to be there. I'm very proud of him."

Unmarried Andrew, 29, was killed in action - alongside 14 other young men in March 1942 when his plane crashed into a hillside in Ireland as they returned from a mission.

A new granite headstone has been commissoned by the CWGC, who spent five years relocating all the unmarked graves.

Iain Anderson, CWGC's Scotland supervisor, said: "Even though our boys were commemorated at another cemetery for the last 60 years when the headstones were removed, it's very special to reinstall the headstones where they lay."²

It was a very moving experience that was attended by several Scottish newspapers and the British Forces Broadcasting service (BFBS). Also, there were two of Mac's cousins, Stuart and Peter, and Peter's daughter, Yvonne. Between us all we did several interviews with various newspapers, as well as a piece to camera for the BFBS. We all went for lunch afterwards and got to know each other a bit as it was the first time we had all met. We remain in contact through the medium of Facebook.

_____

² *Daily Record. (2016).* World War Two airman gets headstone on grave 74 years after he was shot down. *[online] Available at: https://www.dailyrecord.co.uk/news/scottish-news/world-war-two-airman-headstone-9053620 [Accessed 14 Aug. 2024].*

Agnes who was a nurse, 1940

Josephine, Sam, James, and Lena moved to number 2 Rhinsdale Terrace in Baillieston, Glasgow. This was a tenement block of small flats. Josephine did in fact own the whole block, taking the ground floor flat for herself and renting out the flats above. We can assume she was able to afford this as she would have been receiving two widow's pensions from her two marriages. Apparently, she was a very proud landlady and insisted that all the public areas were kept clean and swept, and the front entrance steps scrubbed and mopped daily.

The flats were laid out in a horizontal format with a long corridor from front to back, with the laundry house at the back of the property, which was a shared facility for all the tenants in each block.

Josephine's flat would have had a front parlour for entertaining visitors, and the back room would have had a stove for cooking meals and beds that pulled down from the walls. The toilet was accessed via a corridor at the back of the block.

Sam left home aged nineteen in 1934 to attend Glasgow University to study in the Arts Faculty for the degree of MA (Master of Arts). For some reason, he put his name as Samuel Rentoul Brunton on his matriculation records. It is possible that the Canadian government funded him to attend university as he was the son of a Canadian soldier. The university records show that he studied the following subjects:

1934-1935: English, French

1935-1936: English, Logic, History

1936-1937: Logic, Geography, Scottish History.

Sam didn't graduate from university; in fact, he dropped out in the summer of 1937 at the end of his third year. He only had one more year left to go. In July 1936, the Spanish Civil War had started. Almost 60,000 young men from right across Europe and America responded to the call for help by making their way to Spain to fight on the side of the Spanish Republic led by Francisco Largo Caballero in the battle against the Nationalists, led by the fascist dictator General Franco. They joined the International Brigade.

It all started when Franco launched an uprising aimed at overthrowing the country's democratically elected Republic in a bid to gain political power for himself. The Nationalists were mostly Roman Catholics and were mainly the wealthier people, being landowners and businessmen. The opposition, the Republicans, were made up of urban workers, farmers, and many well-educated middle-class men. The country became politically polarised. Franco was largely successful, and within days of the conflict starting, both sides were calling for foreign military assistance. Britain opted to stay neutral while France opted to support the Spanish Republic. Faced with the possibility of defeat, Franco turned to Nazi Germany and fascist Italy for support. Throughout the war, Hitler and Mussolini provided Franco's army with military armaments. It became the bloodiest war since World War One had ended in 1918. The Nationalist party executed almost 50,000 men, and some 500,000 more became displaced as a result of the conflict. On 28 March 1939, the victorious Nationalists entered Madrid, and the war came to an end. The International Brigade actually disbanded in October 1938. Franco had won and went on to rule Spain until his death in 1975.

Many famous people were involved in the conflict; the author Ernest Hemingway was a war correspondent during this time and went on to write the novel 'For Whom the Bell Tolls', which was published just after the war ended. Another famous author, Laurie Lee, wrote his memoir 'As I Walked Out One Midsummer Morning' about his time fighting in the Republican army, although there are no known official records that place the author in Spain at that time. Even the artist Picasso got involved; he was a supporter of the Republican party and painted the anti-war mural 'Guernica', which was inspired after the Fascists bombed the Basque town of the same name. Picasso never returned to his native country because Franco was then leader for the rest of the artist's life.

More people proportionally went from Scotland than from any other country to fight in the war. They were known as the International Brigades, and MI5 was watching them at the airports and ports and taking note of who was going and returning. It wasn't that easy to get to Spain, as back in the 1930s very few people had a passport. Some managed to get there via France without one, courtesy of the Commonwealth War Graves Commission who used to provide temporary visas for family members so that they could visit the graves of family members killed during the First World War. Many of the fighters slipped away and made their way over the border into Spain. Communism was rife in Scotland at this time, with The Communist Party of Great Britain being founded on 31 July 1920. By the 1930s, Scotland was in an economic depression, and many of the working class became politically active, going on strike to demand better pay and working conditions. There were many protests as pay was poor, unemployment high, and poverty increasing. The plight of the Spanish against fascism was not too dissimilar to what many thought was happening in Scotland. The Communist Party was one of the main recruiters for volunteers for the International Brigades. They generally came from working-class families in trades like coal mining, printing, and construction; in other words, Sam's background.

We believe that Sam joined The Communist Party in 1934, whilst a student at Glasgow University, as the Marx Memorial library in London holds the records of party members from that time.' Like many young political activists, of today he would have felt compelled to try and do something to help, hence his desire to go and fight in Spain.

The National Archives at Kew in London hold almost 4,000 records of the members of the International Brigades. In 2010 these records were made public to coincide with the 75th anniversary of the outbreak of the Spanish Civil War.

Sam would have made his way to the Gran Hotel in Albacete, a city in the southeast-central region of Spain, during the summer of 1937, travelling on his Canadian passport. There he would have been met by other members of the Brigade who had arrived before him and been briefed about what was happening at the time. The first of the International Brigade trainees had arrived on 14 October 1936. Each of the volunteers was allotted three pesetas a day to live on. The British Battalion out there was initially led by First Commander Wilfred MacCartney, a veteran of World War One. Dad would likely have been involved in the fierce Battle of Teruel in December of 1937, as this is the only major battle the British Battalion was involved in while Dad was in Spain.

On the 17th of December 1937, the Republican Army captured the city of Teruel (It was to be recaptured sometime later by the Nationalists). Aware that this was likely to happen, members of the Brigades were moved from

Madrid to a salient high in the Sierra Palomera mountain range, where temperatures dropped to minus twenty at night. There they withstood continuous air attacks made by the Condor Legion, and the Nationalists eventually abandoned their attempt to take Teruel by frontal assault. The battle was bloody, and the rebel aviation could offer little support. The town eventually fell on 7 January 1938. The British contingency took heavy casualties in the battle to defend Teruel in early 1938 and at the battle of the Ebro in July-August 1938. All in all, of the initial 2,000 men of the British Battalion, five hundred were killed, and over one thousand two hundred were seriously wounded. By October 1938, the International Brigades were disbanded. Part of the problem throughout the Civil War was fighting within the Republicans themselves. Half of them were supporters of Stalin, who helped fund the war, and others were anti-Stalinists, favouring the political ideas of Leon Trotsky, and were known as the POUM (The Workers Party of Marxist Unification); also often referred to as Partisans. During the war, this group rapidly gained popularity, although it was not liked by the Spanish Communist Party. Shortly after getting married, the author, George Orwell, headed to Spain to join in the fight; he too was a part of the POUM.

I believe that Dad was also a Partisan, as that is how he referred to himself when he talked about his time in Spain. Many of the leaders of the POUM were killed by Stalinists at the end of the Civil war, a case of communism imploding in on itself.

The only time Dad ever really spoke of his time in Spain was with Bev during a car journey in 1978 when he talked briefly of being in a tree with some other fighters and had Franco in his gunsight and was waiting for the order to shoot. By the time that order came, the opportunity to shoot him had passed.

The last British survivor of the Brigade was Geoffrey Servante, who died in April 2019 at the age of ninety-nine. In 1996, Spain granted citizenship to all Brigadiers, but at that time there were only about six hundred of them left. Since then, Spain has offered citizenship to any descendants of the Brigadiers, providing they can provide proof of their connection.

Had we known it at the time, this would have been useful to Bev as she moved to Spain herself in 2016. Joining The Communist Party can have a long-term effect on your life, as I later learned when we moved to the United States in 2004. Many years earlier, I had been looking for information regarding Dad's time during the Spanish Civil War; many of the records of those who fought are also kept at the Marx Memorial Library in Clerkenwell, London. On a whim, Nigel and I decided to go and visit the library only to be told upon arrival that if we wanted to look at the archive material, I would have to join the party. Having driven in from Hemel Hempstead, rather than make it a wasted journey, I joined the Communist Party...

When we applied for our American visas, I was travelling as a spouse on Nigel's work visa application. It came as a surprise then to receive a letter inviting me to the American Embassy in London for an 'interview'. I couldn't understand why it was only me that got the invitation, but feeling like I had no other choice, I went along to the interview as requested. It turned out that my membership to the Marxist Party several years earlier had come to their attention and they wanted to know if I was basically a political threat to US citizens. I spent a couple of hours with the nice official explaining that I had only joined because I'd driven a long way to look at some dusty documents. Even though I had only signed up for a one-year membership, I continued to receive correspondence from the party for a few years after that. These days, the library is government funded so they can no longer request you join the Marxist party to view anything.

Dad's political beliefs caused another issue twenty-five years after his death when our daughter attended Sandhurst Military Academy. Family members of potential officers have background checks done on them. Anticipating what was coming, I had to write a letter and provide a copy of Dad's death certificate to prove that Dad had died four years before Abbie was born and could not therefore have influenced her political opinions.

His faith in The Communist Party waned after the Hungarian Revolution in 1956. In the October of that year, thousands of protestors took to the streets across Hungary to demand a more democratic political system and to be free of Soviet oppression. In response to this, The Communist Party appointed Imre Nagy, as Prime Minister; he was a former Premier who had previously been kicked out of the party for criticising Stalinist policies.

He did try to promote peace and asked that the Soviets withdraw their troops, which they did. Nagy then tried to abolish the 'one-party rule' – this is when a country is ruled by one political party and the forming of other parties is forbidden. Examples of this today would be North Korea, China, and Vietnam.

Nagy also announced that Hungary was withdrawing from the Warsaw Pact, the Soviet bloc equivalent to NATO.

Russia retaliated, and on 4 November Soviet tanks rolled into Budapest to crush the now National Uprising. Vicious fighting broke out, and nearly 2,500 Hungarians were killed. Nagy sought safety at the Yugoslav Embassy but was captured and executed two years later. The Russians had won and seized back power by brutal force. This use of brutal force and murder of innocent people did not sit well with Dad's political ideology of what The Communist Party was supposed to represent.

The next record we have of Dad is in 1938 when he was found to be working as a window dresser in Edmonton, London. We know this as he has stated his occupation on Ellen's birth certificate. Morag, Ellen's daughter, recalls her mother telling her that Sam had moved to London with his girlfriend, Catherine Shevlin, to study engineering and for Catherine, known as Katie, to study Economics. The two had met while they were both studying at Glasgow University. What we know for sure is that by 1940 they were back living with Josephine at 2 Rhinsdale Terrace in Baillieston, as this is where their second daughter, Josephine, was born.

Dad was then working as an apprentice electric welder on the ships in John Brown's shipyards on the River Clyde where ships such as the Queen Mary and the QE2 were built. Like many of the shipyards at the time, John Brown's was located in the town of Clydebank, in what was known as Queens Quay, situated on the north bank of the River Clyde. The yard was opened in 1871 by the brothers J&G Thomson. John Brown took over the yard in 1897, and it became well-known for building ocean liners as well as warships that were crucial to the war effort.

The role of an electrical welder was to help build and repair ships. Following blueprints, different types of metal were welded to ensure that the structure could withstand the pressure of the ocean. Back in the 1930s, the apprenticeship to become an electrical welder was five years, after which they could become freelancers and work in different shipyards depending on where there was work available. The average wage for the qualified welder was £5-7 a week.

It's hard to imagine being able to support a growing family on that salary and under poor working conditions as well. There were many workers' strikes in the yards over the pay and conditions, particularly for the apprentices, two significant ones being in 1937 and 1952. The apprentices felt that they were drastically underpaid and were being used as cheap labour. Those in the final year of their apprenticeship could be doing the same work as a skilled man but only earn £2 a week. Much of their wages went on transport to get to the docks in the first place. The strikes were supported by the Confederation of Shipbuilding and Engineering unions and they succeeded in getting better pay for the apprentices and ensured that they were unionised and therefore entitled to representation in the future. I am sure Dad would have been at the heart of these strikes and would have fought to ensure fair pay and working conditions for all. It was in the shipyards that his communist ideology flourished, as was the case with many of his peers.

In 1941, the shipyard came under fire in what was known as the Clydebank Blitz when the whole area was heavily bombed by the German Luftwaffe for two nights solidly from the thirteenth to the fifteenth of March, desperately trying to damage production of the warships. About 528 people were killed in the yards over those two nights and another 617 wounded. Men working in the shipyards at the time were exempt from joining the army to fight as their skills were considered too valuable. Being an electric welder on the ships and also being a member of The Communist Party would have meant little chance of Dad being accepted into the British Army. It took him until 1945 to finally be allowed in, by which time he was thirty years old and a father of four.

According to Dad's army service records, he enlisted on 15 March 1945 and spent the next few weeks in the Primary Training Wing before being transferred to the Infantry Training Centre which was then at the Albany Barracks on the Isle Of White. In July, he transferred to RAF Ringway (now Manchester airport) where he commenced his training to become a para. By February 1946, he was on full parachute pay and earned 2 shillings a day. In May that year, he got posted to the fifth Parachute Battalion which had been in Palestine with the sixth Airborne Division since September 1945 in a peace-keeping role as Arab intransigence over the surge of Jewish immigration that followed the Holocaust in Europe had led to the forming of extreme dissident Zionist groups such as IZL (Irgun Zvai Leumi) and the Stern Gang, all seeking to promote their aims through violence.

Dad went out to join the fifth Batallion of the Parachute Regiment at the Tel Litvinsky Camp, which is in Ramat Gan, a city to the east of Tel Aviv. The base was in an ideal position to defend the airfield at RAF Lydda, where troops and military supplies were flown in. The role of the battalion was primarily to support the Palestinian police force by carrying out stop and searches, to man curfew control points, and man physical roadblocks. The battalion was responsible for protecting three police stations at Ra'anana, Ras El Ain, and Petah Tikva. The military base also held Italian Prisoners of War. Lack of staff and heavy security duties left little time for full-scale training, and the battalion was often called out in an internal security role. They assisted local police to set up spot checks and lay ambushes on tracks likely to be used by Jewish terrorists. In August 1946, the battalion took part in Operation Shark, the biggest comb out of Tel Aviv since the explosion in the King David Hotel in Jerusalem, where Jewish terrorists killed more than ninety people, including civilians and British Soldiers, in retaliation for the British occupying Palestine.

In the quarterly report written by Lt Col Churchill, Commander of the Fifth Batallion, he writes: 'Feelings run naturally against the Jews, but this has never been expressed, and in all operations troops have shown the utmost restraint and the battalion appears to have left a favourable impression on the civilians with whom it has come into contact.'

Ironically, during World War Two, the Allies were trying to liberate the Nazi concentration camps, the first being Majdanek in Poland in 1944, and the British (including members of the sixth Airborne Division) liberated Belsen in May 1945 but came under attack from Jewish terrorists in Palestine once the war had ended. The Holocaust had a major effect on the situation in Palestine; during the war, the British restricted the entry into Palestine of European Jews who were trying to flee Nazi persecution. They imposed a limit on Jewish immigration, which provoked an armed Jewish resistance, the Haganah. In late 1945, in response to full-scale riots in Jerusalem and Tel Aviv, British troops had to be deployed to help support the local police. In all, approximately 100,000 British troops were deployed there.

In October 1946, Field Marshal Montgomery visited Lydda airport, which hugely raised morale amongst the troops. This and the impending return to the UK left the battalion in high spirits.

Dad initially had sympathy for the Palestinian people, but after being stationed out there for a year and witnessing atrocities on both sides, he had little sympathy for either. One horror story he talked about was that of finding local women hung up by wire threaded through their nipples. Truly barbaric.

It was whilst stationed out there that Dad first contracted Malaria, which was to flare up on and off throughout the rest of his life.

Dad received two medals; one was the standard War Medal, and the other was a standard issue for having completed a tour of duty in Palestine. Dad handed both of these medals back to the army, saying he didn't want a reward for fighting in a war. I reapplied for these medals a few years ago and now have them on display at home alongside those of both my grandfathers and an uncle. Sadly, we don't know what happened to his red para beret, but I do have his para wings that would have been attached to his beret. Half-brother Peter also followed in his father's footsteps and joined the Parachute Regiment as a young man.

In February 2018, Nigel, Abbie, Leo, and I went on a history trip to Israel, known as Palestine when Dad was there. It was one of the most interesting and informative trips we have been on. We stayed in Tel Aviv, a vibrant cosmopolitan city with beautiful beaches. Two miles south of Tel Aviv is the ancient city of Jaffa, where Jews and Arabs live side by side in harmony. We experienced nothing but warmth and wonderful hospitality in both cities and really enjoyed exploring the history of both, and the food was amazing! Nigel managed to find us a guide willing to take us into the West Bank to visit Jerusalem, some forty miles away. It all felt a little cloak and dagger, and I remember telling Abbie to make sure she had no ID on her that would identify her as British military. We were picked up outside our hotel and then driven to a discreet layby outside a convent where we were told to wait for another car that would then take us through the checkpoint into the West Bank. A car with Jewish number plates is not allowed into Bethlehem, so we had to be transferred into one with Arab number plates. We seemed to be waiting a long time; Abbie was getting increasingly concerned and was messaging her brother, back in the UK, details of the car we were travelling in. Eventually, the car arrived, and we switched over. Our new driver was Syrian and called Saied, and invited us to his house in Bethlehem for tea! Firstly, we had to get through checkpoint 300, where the car was approached by heavily armed guards and searched thoroughly, and Saied was questioned about who we were and what we were doing. At last, we were through, and the first thing we saw was the Walled Hotel, owned by the artist Banksy, who is obviously a Palestinian sympathiser. His distinctive artwork can be seen all along the checkpoint wall.

After cups of tea at Saied's house, we were taken by his cousin for a tour of Bethlehem. A strange experience. Nativity Square has the Church of Nativity, which is built upon the site of the stable where Jesus is alleged to have been born. The stable would've actually been a cave back in those days, and the area can be accessed via steep steps below the church floor. In the nearby Church of Ascension, which is built upon the site where Jesus allegedly hung on the cross, there remains an original cave of the time that you can crawl down into to see what conditions would've been like at the time of the alleged holy birth. Opposite the church is a huge mosque! All churches in the Holy Land are split into three sections, one each for Roman Catholics, Greek Orthodox, and the Armenian Apostolic. As they all share the same church, then each religion had to choose their own Christmas Day. Christianity got 25 Dec, the Armenians got 6 January, and the Greek Orthodox 7 January. Each section is visibly very different from the other and each has its own religious figurehead, all of whom can be seen at the church entrance greeting visitors. Whilst in the crypt below the church, which is where the supposed stable was, we became aware of shouting coming from above, and we were all hurried out of the church by officials. I recall feeling somewhat alarmed and wanting to get out as quickly as possible to a place of safety for us all. As it was, we were being turfed out in favour of some religious bigwig who had turned up with an enormous cavalcade of security.

After Bethlehem, we were driven to a drop-off point in Jerusalem where we were told to wait at the bottom of some steps for our guide, Shai, to find us. The steps led to a new shopping centre; Shai referred to it as the most hopeful point in Jerusalem as it is the only place where you will see both Jews and Arabs peacefully in the same vicinity.

We spent eight hours exploring and learning about the city of Jerusalem with Shai, who was so knowledgeable on the history, religion, and politics of the city. Sadly, as a young gay man, he cannot live in the city he was born in, and so lives in the less conservative city of Tel Aviv.

Jerusalem is divided into four quarters: The Christian, the Armenian, the Jewish, and the Muslim. The Jewish section is ultra-Orthodox, the Armenian section is the smallest, and there's no entry to outsiders unless your surname is Kardashian! We spent all of our time exploring the Muslim quarter under which runs a series of hidden tunnels through which people are smuggled. The narrow cobbled streets are heavily patrolled by armed police, and attacks are not uncommon. There are bomb detonator containers dotted around the more religious areas, a white circular steel structure with a door, used for containing unexploded bombs in the event of an attack.

What was once the Temple Mount where Jesus was said to have prayed is now a mosque called Al-Aqsa, used by the Muslims except for one small section of the outer wall which is now known as the Western Wall or Wailing Wall where the Jewish people come to pray. When we went to see the wall, Abbie and I were not allowed in the same section as the men. We were required to cover our heads when we approached the wall. Shai advised us to reach up as high as we could to feel how smooth the stone is after centuries of pilgrims have worn it smooth with their hands. In every nook and cranny are slips of paper on which prayers are written. In both sections, there are bookcases filled with copies of the Torah. The sound of people wailing and the sight of men maniacally rocking was really quite unnerving. I remember trying not to catch Abbie's eye as I had finished looking at the wall. It became apparent that it was taboo to turn your back to it, and so I realised I was going to have to walk backwards to where Abbie stood. The whole area was strewn with chairs and tables and bookshelves, and I knew Abbie was getting the giggles knowing that I was likely to stumble and fall over. I can hardly walk forwards without stumbling over. It was all totally mind-blowing; my mind was buzzing with all we had learned for weeks after we returned home. Sadly, I cannot imagine there ever being a peaceful outcome for the Muslim or Jewish communities here; they are intent on killing each other and all in the name of religion.

In June 1946, Dad was promoted to the rank of Education Sergeant and found himself back in the UK, admitted to Tidworth Military Hospital in Wiltshire with serious shrapnel injuries to his leg. The hospital was built in 1907 near the army training grounds of Salisbury Plains and had two to three hundred beds. It eventually closed in 1977, three years after the singer James Blunt was born there, who also went on to become a serving officer in the British Army. Despite searching through the war diaries of his battalion, I

90

have been unable to establish how and where in Palestine this injury occurred. It was certainly serious enough for him not to be discharged from hospital care for over a year. He walked with a slight limp from that injury for the rest of his life, particularly when the weather was very cold.

The Sixth Airborne Division eventually left Palestine in 1948 after the Israeli Declaration of Independence was proclaimed on 14 May of the same year. Israel became a state and the British Mandate over Palestine expired, so the British withdrew.

The airborne units were disbanded except for the Second Parachute Brigade, of which the Fifth Battalion was part.

Dad was discharged from the army on 31 July 1947, aged thirty-eight years. His and Katie's third son, Edward, was born the following year.

The four boys

From left to right: Peter, David, Edward and Sam

CHAPTER 8: LIFE AFTER THE ARMY

In 1950, according to family folklore in both families, Dad was advised to get out of Scotland for his own safety. It is believed that he had angered the leaders of the Scottish Nationalists to the point that his personal safety was threatened. Despite looking extensively for evidence of some kind of documented disagreement, I can find nothing to substantiate any such threat. Unfortunately, this means that we don't know what led Dad to leave his beloved Scotland and his young family, and to head south into England. It was quite possible that he was simply looking for work in the post-war era with a salary sufficient to provide for his family.

What we are able to establish is that after leaving the army, Dad got a job as a safety inspector with Whessoe Engineering. At that time, they were suppliers of chemical, oil, and nuclear plant and instrumentation, and they were based in Darlington. They still are but these days they design and build low temperature and cryogenic storage and handling facilities.

In 1951, the job took him to work for Stanlow Oil Refinery in Ellesmere Port. To this day, whenever I travel to Chester, to see Mum, I drive past the refinery and I am reminded that Dad helped facilitate the building of what looks like two giant golf balls there, which are visible from the M56. He moved into a lodging house in Westminster Road in the town with landlords Nora and Bill; who also worked for Whessoe. He lived there from Monday to Friday and returned to the family in Glasgow at weekends. It was through his landlords that he met Mum, Joyce Swinburn, then a twenty-one-year-old student nurse. Dad was thirty-nine years old. They began dating, attending local dances and going out on Joyce's motorbike, often escorted by

Joyce's older brother, Jack, who was dating Val, a friend of Joyce.

Whessoe offered Dad the opportunity to go out to Australia to work, but he declined the offer and Bill went in his place, and that is where he and Nora lived for the rest of their lives. Mum's brother, Jack, also moved out to Australia, and they all remained good friends.

Several months passed until one day, Joyce's mother met her at the train station on her way back from the hospital, looking very flustered. She told her daughter that there was a lady at the house who said she was Sam's wife.

Katie must have had her suspicions about Sam, or maybe they had talked about it and she had caught the train from Glasgow to Ellesmere Port to confront Joyce and to tell her that Sam wasn't hers to have. I have to say, when Mum told me this, and it's one of the few things she has told me, I was impressed with Katie; she was fighting for her marriage. Good on her. It must have been a very awkward evening for them all as there was only one train a day to Glasgow, so Katie actually ended up staying at my grandparents' house overnight before catching the train back up to Glasgow the following day.

Joyce, our mum, was bereft; she'd had no idea that Sam was married, and so she ended the relationship. Apparently, it was our maternal grandmother who, three months later, went to find Sam and told him how miserable Joyce was and if he was sure Joyce was what he wanted, then he had to end things in Scotland. I imagine that was a huge decision for my religious grandma to make as it would have gone against the teachings of the Bible.

Morag recalls her mum, Ellen, telling her that initially, Sam returned to Glasgow to see his children weekly, then fortnightly, which became monthly until the visits tailed off altogether. Mum tells us that she did send regular postal cheques to a post office in Baillieston, but then claims she thought there were only two children. How can you spend thirty-five years with a man and not know how many children he has?

PETER

When Dad left, I was six years old. It was in 1951. At that time, we were living at 24 South Scott Street in Baillieston. This was a two-bedroom upper quarter villa and was too small for us all. Staying there eventually entitled us to a bigger house because of the overcrowding, and in 1955, when I was ten years old, we moved to 34 Caledonia Road in Baillieston. This was a newly built house with three bedrooms and gardens at the front and back. My mother lived in that house for the rest of her life.

Granny Brunton had a massive involvement in our upbringing and always had a great love and respect for my mother. She constantly told her she was doing an excellent job with our upbringing and education. We all went to high school and university.

After Dad left, Granny Brunton had no contact with him, saying she would never speak to him again, and as far as I know, it stayed that way. We saw Granny Brunton two to three times a week and every Sunday for ten a.m. Mass at St Bridget's Roman Catholic Church.

During the summer holidays, my mother had to continue to work, so Granny Brunton looked after us four boys on a daily basis. Granny made the best ham ribs and dumplings in the whole of Scotland!

Over the next decade, Sam and Joyce moved around the country with Dad's job, living in a mobile home that Whessoe literally transferred on a huge truck with each new contract. In 1959 they moved to Milford Haven where Dad worked at the local Oil Refinery. On the campsite were lots of other young families, and this is where they first met Marion, yet another Scot, and Eileen, from Bournemouth, whose husbands also worked at the Refinery. These two ladies went on to become two of Mum's closest friends. A friendship trio that lasted for the rest of their lives. Mum told me recently about there being a workers' strike at the Refinery and Aunty Marion banging on the door, shouting for Mum to put the television on as Dad was on the news speaking up for the workers' rights.

Beverley was born in 1961 after Mum had travelled back up to Ellesmere Port to have the support of her own mother and sister. Bev was named after a young girl Mum had nursed years previously who had been in the hospital with polio and whom Mum had become very fond of.

After Milford Haven, Mum said she received a phone call from Dad saying he had got a job in Dublin and for her to get the next ferry over to Ireland to join him. From Dublin, they moved into digs on the Antrim Road in Belfast. Mum hated living there; the streets had crowds of angry young men who were very threatening towards the English. The other people in the house would check the road was clear of them to ensure it was safe for Mum to leave the house. This was not a great environment in which to raise a child, but they were there until Bev turned four when they moved back to England, this time to Berkeley in Gloucestershire. Dad was then working at the nuclear reactor at Oldfield. Once again, they were living in a mobile home provided by the company. By now, Mum had her beloved Tosca, the keeshond dog who was intensely loyal to her and travelled in the sidecar of Mum's motorbike.

Bev started school in Berkeley, and so Mum went back to work part-time. Up until then, she had been doing seasonal work such as picking strawberries and mashing up grapes and says she was sending postal cheques to a post office in Bo'ness for Katie every week to help pay for the children. Ellen and Peter have both said they were never aware of any money arriving. If Mum thought there were only two children, as she claims she thought there were, then any money she sent was woefully inadequate.

Bev developed a broad Gloucestershire accent and caused much hilarity with their neighbours as she called Dad 'Sam,' never having heard anyone else call him 'Dad.'

On 18 December 1967, I arrived in the world. I was born in Clatterbridge Hospital on the Wirral and started life being called Candice, after the actress Candice Bergen. Apparently, had I been a boy, I would have been called Stuart. Thankfully, it was left to Dad to register my birth and by the time he got to the Registrar's office, I was a Fiona!

Dad was now working back at Stanlow Oil Refinery in Ellesmere Port, and he decided it was time they settled down in one place, much to Mum's annoyance. The story goes that Mum looked at 8 Dawn Gardens in Ellesmere Port by torchlight and grumpily agreed to the purchase. We lived in that house until I was four years old, Bev attending a tiny primary school in Childer Thornton where Mum's sister lived, a suburb of Ellesmere Port. According to Mum, Dad at this time was part of the Liverpool branch of the Communist Party, although there was a smaller branch at the local Vauxhall factory. Unfortunately, the Liverpool records now only date back to 1960, so I have been unable to find any membership details.

Before I started primary school, we moved to Saughall; we were going up in the world. Mum and Dad were polar opposites when it came to politics. As I've already mentioned, Mum had been raised in the Salvation Army and was very conservative in her views; she still is. Dad was a communist (socialist), so you can imagine the arguments they had. Growing up, we were told, by Mum, that communism was a bad word and that it wasn't to be used outside of the home. Come the national elections, Mum would have posters of whoever the Conservative leader of the time would be, displayed in the lounge window. On my walk home from school, I would know if Dad was due home that day as she would swap the poster for that of the opposition Labour Party Leader. He wasn't at home every night like most dads were, as between the ages of me being nine to twelve, he was living and working in Darlington in the North East from Monday to Friday.

When we met Ellen, we talked about Dad's communist beliefs, and she told us that as a child, she would be taken to secret members' meetings in cafes across Glasgow. Dad would put her in the front of the cafe with a treat of some kind to keep a lookout for any police that may come in. She would have been a good decoy as they wouldn't have expected a child to be present during an illicit meeting of political activists.

Glasgow at this time was known as Red Clydeside as the communist party became a popular choice for those in the working class and who were opposed to Britain's participation in the First World War, feeling it was a decision made by the English 'toffs' in Whitehall and not in the best interest of the working-class population who would suffer the most losses during the conflict. In Glasgow alone, some 200,000 men from the city joined up to fight, and 17,695 lost their lives.

As children, Dad never ever laid a hand on either Bev nor I, and almost always managed to diffuse a potential escalating drama with humour. He did, however, always teach me that if someone was to hit you once, I was to then try and walk away, but if they were going to do it again, to make sure I hit them hard enough that they didn't get up again. I remember one incident when I must have been five or six years old and had been playing outside with my pram and dolls. A local boy, Michael Hughes, who was a little older than me, kicked my pram over, buckling the wheels. I pushed my wonky pram home in tears and told Dad what had happened. He walked me back to where Michael was still playing and, standing behind Michael, pinned his arms to his side and told me to kick the boy as hard as I could. That, he said, was how to deal with a bully. Imagine now if a parent did that to another person's child.

He was a good Dad to Bev and I, which makes it so difficult to reconcile the Dad that we had was the one who walked out on a wife and six children, leaving them all to fend for themselves. Maybe it was guilt that made him try so much harder when it came to being a parent for us. I do believe that Mum probably made it increasingly difficult for him to visit his children, believing that he should only focus on her, Bev and I. What on earth went through his mind when we visited Aunty Lena in Edinburgh or took holidays in Oban and in Glen Lyon, knowing that his first family was so nearby? We will never know. I find it hard to forgive him for being such a weak man after everything Bev and I have learned on this journey. These days it just wouldn't be a scandalous affair, and yet Mum still refuses to be open with us. I think that, like Dad and Lena, Mum had hoped to take Dad's secret to the grave with her. She is the first to admit that she is able to 'compartmentalise' things she wants to know and things she can choose to ignore. Initially, I think she was simply a very naïve and impressionable young adult who was flattered by the attention of a handsome, much older man.

Dad must have tried to divorce Katie, but due to her Roman Catholic beliefs, she refused. The Divorce Reform

Act of 1969 meant that Dad could then get his divorce as he and Katie had been separated for more than five years. Bev did discover that our parents eventually married in 1977 and that Mum had our birth certificates changed so that we no longer appeared as being illegitimate. Katie died in 2001, aged eighty-three, in a Nursing Home in Airdrie. Her death was registered by son Sam and still had Dad's name and occupation on it as her spouse.

I can remember the phone call from Aunty Lena in 1986 when she told Dad that their mother had died. His one-word response was: 'Good.' I don't think they ever spoke again after Dad walked out. I do wonder if he would have felt differently towards her had he known the hardships she had suffered in order to keep her family together. It must have been so upsetting for her to see him give up so easily on his. Granny Brunton supported Dad's wife and children throughout their lives before dying on 12 February 1986 in St Mary's Hospital in Lanarkshire, following a stroke.

Our Mum still insists that Dad never forgave his mum for denouncing her marriage to his father and that is why he never spoke to her. This cannot be true because we know that he continued to live with her or in her tenement building right up to the time he left Scotland. I think it more likely that Granny Brunton could not find it in herself to forgive Dad and that it was she who chose to never have contact with him again.

Sam's wife, May, told me that she only ever heard Dad's name mentioned once, and it was during a discussion between two of Dad's sons when talking about the army, and one of them said:

'Our Dad fought in two wars, but he never fought for us.'

EPILOGUE

Dad, I think will remain an enigma to us all. There are so many questions from both his first family and from Bev and I. Sadly, it is unlikely that we will ever get the answers now. The questions I would most like the answers to are why he left Scotland, was it for his own safety and that of his family, and if so, where was the threat coming from and why did he not try harder to maintain a relationship with his children? I totally understand that marriages break down but that is not the fault of the children. They are the victims in this scenario. Mum has said that for many years he carried a photograph of Ellen in his wallet, so he obviously did care about them. I don't know what happened to that photograph, and I have never seen it. I would like to know the truth behind the breakdown of his relationship with Granny Brunton and whether or not Dad and James were actually full siblings, given that she was 7 months pregnant when she married Sam Brunton senior.

Something else that some of the family have queried is regarding his trips to Peking and North Korea. Given his political beliefs and his previous involvement with the Spanish Civil War, was he there for legitimate reasons? Is it possible he was spying, and if so, for whom? The Cold War was at its peak between 1948 and 1953. North Korea contributed to it when it invaded South Korea on June 25th, 1950. However, this was over twenty years before Dad was there, and his interest in communism had waned considerably after Russia invaded Hungary in 1956. I do imagine that he could well have been under surveillance by British Intelligence Organisations at the time, and I did apply for information from these organisations under the Freedom of Information Act 2000 whilst carrying out research for this book. The email responses I received from them all informed me that the Intelligence Agencies were exempt from releasing information regarding individuals under the Act in the interest of public and national safety. So no answers are forthcoming from these sources.

At the end of this search for the truth, I personally am left feeling conflicted in many ways. I carry guilt that I had a fun and caring Dad and grew up in a happy and secure environment but that it was not the same for Dad's first six children. I feel resentment and disappointment towards both of my parents for keeping this secret and therefore denying us a relationship with our half-siblings. It saddens me that I never got to have an adult relationship with Dad. Although I was twenty years old when he died, his brain had been slowly decaying since I was fifteen. There were so many conversations that never got spoken.

Ultimately, I feel so disappointed that a man I adored and looked up to shirked all of his responsibilities by walking away from six young children who equally adored and depended on him. That, I find, is unforgivable.

FAMILY TREE

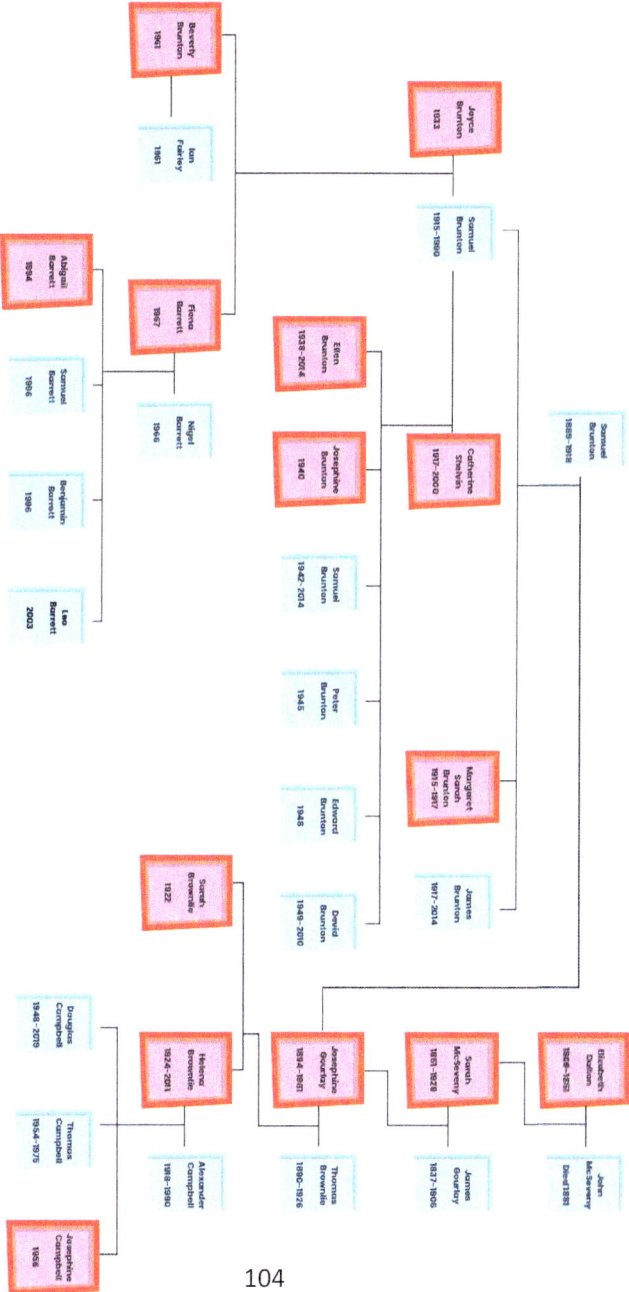

I never told Mum that I was writing this book. She had made the conscious decision to never be truthful or open with me, so, ultimately, I chose not to share with her that I was putting Dad's life story down on paper. I loved my mum and did not want to cause any hurt or embarrassment to her, especially as she was very elderly at the time of my writing this book. I thought I would get away with her never finding out about its existence. It is for the benefit of my own children and for Dad's first family that I wrote this so that they may understand a little of their own history.

In the end, I didn't need to tell Mum, as she passed away suddenly in October 2023.

RESOURCES

1. www.scotlandspeople.co.uk
2. www.ancestry.com
3. www.britannica.com
4. www.iwm.org.uk
5. www.thinkspain.com
6. www.theheraldscotland.com
7. www.clydewaterfront.com
8. The National Archives, Kew, London
9. The Marx Memorial Library, Clerkenwell, London
10. Picasso Museum, Malaga, Spain
11. Merseyside Records Office
12. The Home Office
13. Fairfield Heritage Centre, Glasgow
14. Glasgow University Archives
15. The People's History Museum, Manchester

Printed in Great Britain
by Amazon